The Reader Writes the Story

Canadian and World Short Fiction

The Reader Writes the Story

Canadian and World Short Fiction

Marilyn Chapman / John Barnes

Prentice-Hall Canada Inc.

To Farrell and Angela Chapman
And to Marg for understanding, patience and support

Canadian Cataloguing in Publication Data

Main entry under title:

The Reader writes the story: Canadian and
world short fiction

ISBN 0-13-763509-5

1. Short stories, Canadian (English).*   2. Short stories.   3. Canadian
fiction (English) - 20th century*.   4. Fiction - 20th century.   I.
Chapman, Marilyn, date-   .   II. Barnes, John, date-   .

PS8321.R43 1991   C813'.010805   C91-094666-3
PR9197.32.R43 1991

Prentice-Hall, Inc., Englewood Cliffs, New Jersey
Prentice-Hall International, Inc., London
Prentice-Hall of Australia, Pty., Ltd., Sydney
Prentice-Hall of India Pvt., Ltd., New Delhi
Prentice-Hall of Japan, Inc., Tokyo
Prentice-Hall of Southeast Asia (PTE) Ltd., Singapore
Editora Prentice-Hall do Brasil Ltda., Rio de Janeiro
Prentice-Hall Hispanoamericana, S.A., Mexico

ISBN 0-13-763509-5

Research and Marketing Manager: David Steele
Managing Editor: Alan Simpson
Editors: Susan Sopcek, Mary Beth Leatherdale, Linda Bishop
Production Editor: Diane Lapena
Production Coordinator: Crystale Chalmers
Permissions: Sharon Houston and Robyn Craig
Text and Cover Design: Monica Kompter
Composition and Typesetting: Hermia Chung
Cover: *La Perspective Amoureuse (View of Love)* by René Magritte.
          Copyright 1991 Charly Herscovici/ARS, N.Y. Reproduced by
          permission of ARS, N.Y.

Printed and bound in Canada by Webcom Limited
1 2 3 4 5 6 W 97 96 95 94 93 92

Policy Statement
Prentice-Hall Canada Inc., School Division, and the editors of *The Reader
Writes the Story* are committed to the publication of instructional materi-
als that are as bias-free as possible. This anthology was evaluated for
bias prior to publication.

The editors and publisher also recognize the importance of appro-
priate reading levels and have therefore made every effort to ensure the
highest degree of readability in the anthology. The content has been
selected and organized at a level suitable to the intended audience.

Contents

Acknowledgements

Gayle Rosen cast a candid eye and assisted in more ways than she realized. Our thanks to her and to Jennifer Adams for the drama unit, Lesley Elliott for the unit on teaching stories from other cultures, and George Pepall for the debating unit. We are also grateful to Anaheeta Bharucha, Craig Campbell, and Aria Ratnam for their assistance. A special thanks to Farrell Chapman who, in spite of sun and sand and sea, read and read and read. Finally, thanks to Rob Douglas and Jack Nahrgang, who picked up pieces, and read and inspired.

Our gratitude is also extended to Prentice-Hall, particularly David Steele and Alan Simpson for initiating the project and to Susan Sopcek, Mary Beth Leatherdale, Chelsea Donaldson, and Diane Lapena for their fine editorial work.

Prentice-Hall Canada Inc. wishes to express its sincere appreciation to the following Canadian educators for contributing their time and expertise during the development of this text.

Evelyn Bayefsky, Librarian, Don Mills, ON

Mark Brubacher, Consultant for Student-Centred Learning, Board of Education for the City of York, ON

Patricia McIntosh, English Department Head, Sir Winston Churchill School, Vancouver, BC

Jill Kedersha McClay, University of Alberta, Edmonton, AB

Phyllis B. Schwartz, English Department Head, Lord Byng Secondary School, Vancouver, BC

Inclusion of a person in this list does not indicate that person's endorsement of the text.

To the Reader

Student: *"The Reader Writes the Story."* You're kidding, right?

Editors: What do you mean?

Student: Well, everyone knows the *author* writes the story, not the *reader*.

Editors: Hmm...... maybe the title doesn't make much sense at first, but think about stories for a minute—the kind we tell every day. Let's say you went to a dance or a game on the weekend with a bunch of other kids. Your best friend, who couldn't go, asks you to tell her how it was. "Great!" you say. Would your friend say, "Good," and start talking about something else?

Student: No way! She would want to know all the details— who was there, and what happened.

Editors: So, you tell her the details. You describe what happened, giving her your version of the event. Now she asks someone else to describe it. Would he describe it exactly the way you did?

Student: Well, no—not exactly.

Editors: What if she asks five different people? Wouldn't they each have a slightly different story?

Student: Of course. Now I see what you mean. Even though it was the same dance or game, everyone who was there would have seen it in a slightly different way.

Editors: Exactly! Now let's say a whole group of you get together to talk about this event. Would you enjoy telling stories about it and listening to others tell their stories?

Student: Yeah, it might be fun.

Editors: When we tell *our* stories and listen to other people tell *theirs*, we begin to see things we didn't see before. This helps us to clarify things and make sense of what happened.

Student: Okay, but what does that have to do with the title of this book?

Editors: Well, first of all, let's say that you and some other people read the first story, "**My Name Is Angie**." Would you agree that what interests you about the story wouldn't necessarily interest others?

Student: Yeah. It's kind of like watching a movie: some people like one part best and some like another. How come?

Editors: Maybe it's because when each of us reads a story, or sees a movie, the words and ideas get filtered through all the things past and present that we have ever heard, seen, or experienced.

Student: I don't understand.

Editors: Well, we've all grown up in different families, met different people, visited different places, and accumulated different memories, right? So we feel differently about things and respond to them in different ways.

Student: And when we go somewhere like a dance or a game, the same kind of thing happens?

Editors: In a way. We all respond to experiences differently, and reading a story is an experience. If, for instance, you and your friends read a story that focuses on being liked by your peers, as "**My Name Is Angie**" does, then each of you will have your own feelings about it because each of you feels differently about being liked by your peers. Even though you all read the same *words*, each of you will respond to them in a slightly different way. In a sense, you will all read a slightly different story because . . .

Student: I get it! In a way, the reader *does* write the story! Now the title's beginning to make sense.

Editors: Okay, now let's assume that you and your friends start sharing your ideas about the story. Are you likely to agree on every point?

Student: Probably not.

Editors: Do you think it might be interesting to talk about your different reactions?

Student: Maybe. It would be kind of like talking about a movie or a basketball game, I guess. Everyone would notice something different. You could exchange ideas about the plot and the characters and everything.

Editors: When we start sharing ideas and talking them over with others a lot happens. Trying to find the words to express our ideas often makes them clearer; we begin to understand ourselves better. And when we listen to other people . . .

Student: We begin to understand *them* better. I get it. You know, some of the things you said about "My Name Is Angie" sounded kind of interesting. I think I'll read it.

Editors: It's a good story. Hope you enjoy it.

My Name Is Angie

BEVERLEY TERRELL-DEUTSCH

I t would happen without warning, but Angie did not know that. Unaware, she carefully put the finishing touches on her pale pink nails and checked her hair once more—ready for another day. Her black stirrup pants and just-right, oversized hot pink sweater were the result of hours of shopping with her mother. Planning and choosing her wardrobe were serious issues for Angie. How she looked really mattered a lot; it was something she could be good at if she tried.

Her grades were a different matter, really a worry—four failures on her last report card. Her parents were understanding and didn't push her; they knew she was struggling and doing as well as she could.

School had never come easy for Angie. Many times she had endured humiliation at the mercy of her classmates. She still cringed when she recalled the terrible year she had spent in Grade Four with Richard and Ian Carson, the twins. They had chanted, "Angie, Angie, can't pass can she!" over and over, dancing and hooting around her with the wicked cruelty of young children. If she thought about it too much, even now, more than five whole years later, Angie could still feel the sting of impending tears.

She had spent a second year in that grade, a second year with the same impatient, frightening teacher who really didn't seem to have much time for her. She had hated and dreaded the Times Tables Drills the most. She could never keep them all straight. Every Thursday night she had practised for hours with her mother; Drill Day was always Friday. The teacher made each child take a turn standing at the front of the class. The children in their seats would, one by one, up and down the rows, hurl out a times table at the one up front. Anyone making a mistake had to recite, out loud, the corrected version a hundred times and then write it out another hundred times for homework.

Angie always asked an easy one, like "two times three," in hopes that maybe the others would ask her easy ones, too. Some did, but lots of them showed off, asking really hard ones from the eight or nine times table. Often, Angie had spent most of the weekend with one or other of her parents sitting encouragingly next to her as she labored, hour after hour, writing out times tables at the dining-room table.

At last, the year and the Times Tables Drills were over and Angie found, with something like surprise, that she had ultimately profited from the misery. She had memorized all of the times tables, every single one. Well, she still was a little shaky about "eight times nine" unless she first recited in her head, "eight times eight is sixty-four," but then "eight times nine is seventy-two" usually came. If it didn't, she could always count on her fingers eight more than sixty-four, but she had to be sure to keep her fingers still as she counted, just pressing them gently against the desk top or her thigh. She didn't want anyone to see her fingers moving and guess what she was doing. She didn't want to be laughed at.

Angie had learned long ago to cover up a lot; by pretending she was sure of herself, by not letting others know how she really felt or what she didn't know, she attempted to avoid censure and ridicule. What she did most of the time was to sit in class very quiet and very still and never, absolutely never, catch the teacher's eye. In this way, she tried to quietly disappear. Since starting high school, things were a little better because she was called on in class only occasionally and even then, the teachers didn't know her name. They usually singled her out by referring to "the blonde girl with the blue jacket on," or whatever.

Angie almost always knew when she was about to be

called upon. She could tell, even without glancing up, if the teacher was looking her way by the directness of the sound of the voice. Then there would be a long pause as they tried to think of her name and couldn't. Angie's heart always started pounding during this silent pause.

Once, while waiting for the fatal words, with eyes down, staring at sweaty hands, she was surprised to find that one part of her panic-frozen brain was busy reciting the times tables in an objective, disconnected sort of way. That day she had discovered a trick, a life-saving mind game. If she just made herself think about something other than how afraid she was, she found she could sort of sidestep the panic. It was still there, but just because it was there didn't mean she had to look it full in the face—she could look in another direction. She learned to turn to the unchanging pattern of the times tables.

Strange how an old enemy had become one of her best friends. The multiplication tables were the perfect soother. She recited them starting at "one times one" and worked right up to "twelve times twelve" if she had to, each one rolling off in memory like a familiar name, a favorite pebble turned over and over, smooth and round and cool. Of course, if the teacher actually asked her a question, the numbers fell away as panic flooded back again, wide-eyed and trembling. But some comfort, even if short-lived, was better than none.

"Angie, darling, breakfast is ready!" her mother's voice cut across her thoughts.

"Coming, Mom."

Angie lived just a few miles from the farmer who drove the school bus. He was a little late this morning; the roads were clogged with snow and ice from last night's storm, but finally the bus lumbered into view and Angie climbed on. She sat alone, as usual. There weren't many kids on yet, but as they got closer to the school, pickup stops became more frequent and soon the bus was almost full. Angie had never yet had a boy sit next to her. It was something she dreaded. Every day as the seats gradually filled up, she prayed that it would be a girl who took the seat beside her.

"Please God, don't let him sit here. Oh, please don't let him!" She always watched what was happening in the window's reflection beside her.

"Please, God, make it be a girl...make it be a girl!"

So far, it had worked. It worked again this morning. Alex sat beside her—beautiful, clever, popular Alex. Alex was vice-president of the Student Council this year. Angie shifted a shy sideways glance to see whether a smile would be returned. It wouldn't; Alex was already busy, her head bent into her French text. Angie looked back out the window to the reflection of Alex coasting along in the air a few feet away.

"She's so pretty and so smart...love the dangling pom-pom on her toque...love how it dances when we hit a bump...heard her tell her friends her grandma knit it for her. She's got so many friends, girls and boys, too...bet she even goes out with boys. She seems so brave around them, always laughing and having fun. Maybe if Mom knit me a toque with a dangling pompom..." Angie drifted off into her thoughts, still looking out her window, sometimes at Alex's composed studious reflection, sometimes out past that to the fence posts, pastureland and trees sliding by.

Angie knew the landscape by heart, each grove of trees, which fields had sheep and which had cattle. She had read the same mailboxes and gazed at the same farmhouses every day except weekends for almost six months now. She found the familiar journey reassuring in its sameness and predictability. It was a quiet time for her to think her own thoughts with no out-side demands—a quiet time to build up her resources and pre-pare for the day ahead.

Now they were at the top of the last big hill before the road swooped down and over the bridge on the final lap before reaching the school. All the pickups had been made. No more stops now till they were there.

Angie felt the bus gathering speed as it rumbled down the hill toward the bridge. Anyone would think they'd have made the bridge a little sturdier over such an angry and hostile-looking stretch of water. It was always frothing and foaming, leaping up around the scarred banks as if intent on escaping. Even now, in the dead of winter, the stretch upriver from the bridge remained open, lashing and tugging at the great, frozen chunks it had earlier thrown up in disgust on the banks. Further down, below the bridge, the surface had reluctantly frozen, but the heart of the angry blackness was alive, just inches below, ready to snatch away anything or anyone foolish enough to come close.

Any second now and they'd be on the bridge. Angie always hated the hollow rumble they made as they crossed. It made the bridge seem even less substantial somehow.

If it hadn't been for the driver's quick reflexes when they hit the patch of ice on the bridge, the bus would have been right over the side. But, he did all the right things. He steered into the skid, then corrected; steered into the skid the other direction and corrected again, but it wasn't quite enough. There was a horrible, jarring crash; metal being crushed; glass shattering. Finally, they slid to a quivering stop, only the back wheels left on the bridge. The front third of the bus was hanging at an angle, out over the wild water below. A sudden gust of wind moaned through the smashed guardrails and set the bus rocking, like a teeter-totter, softly rocking in a terrifying caricature of all the lovely, gentle things usually associated with being rocked.

Not a sound. Complete, frozen silence.

"Don't anybody move! Just sit real still, everybody. We're okay as long as we just hold tight." It was the driver's voice, a hoarse, trembling voice trying not to tremble. Angie recognized the sound of fear. She had heard it enough in her own voice many times.

"Just sit still, kids, we'll be okay. Just don't panic. A transport truck has seen us; he's stopped; he'll radio for help. Just hang on kids..."

Angie was pushed forward and sideways by the angle of the bus. She could clearly see the river rushing by below, deep and dark and waiting...

"I'll just sit very, very still and be very quiet..." This terrified animal posture was nothing new to Angie; she did it every day in every class.

Awful, little, strangled, throaty noises from somewhere nearby..."I can't! I can't!...let me out...I want to go, I want to get out!" The voice rose almost to a scream. It was Alex. She started to get up; a shudder from the sudden movement ran the whole length of the bus. Her books slithered from her lap, hit the floor and slid several seat lengths forward, down toward the gently dipping and swaying nose of the bus. Finally, catching on something, they stopped.

Alex stopped too, halfway standing, frozen. Alex on the edge of panic. Others were, too, Angie could feel it. Panic threatening—crackling through the bus, alive and awesome. They weren't listening to the driver. They were too afraid. But Angie knew how to handle fear, even this kind of fear.

She reached out and took Alex's hand, gently pulling her back down into the seat. Still holding her hand, in a small but distinct voice, Angie spoke out.

"One times one is one; one times two is two; one times three is three; one times four is four..." She spoke with the same steady rhythm she had used to ease her own panic so many times before. Were they listening?

"...One times eleven is eleven; one times twelve is twelve; two times one is two; two times two is four; two times three is six..." on and on, her voice steady and strong. They listened; it was hypnotic. "...Six times six is thirty-six; six times seven is forty-two..." Silence except for Angie's voice. "...Eight times eight is sixty-four; eight times nine is seventy-two...."

Everyone listened, following the rhythmic cadences of her voice, their minds locked into the pattern of numbers, their minds turned away from fear. Some silently moved their lips in time with Angie. "...Twelve times seven is eighty-four; twelve times eight is ninety-six..." On she went, never faltering; steady, perfect rhythm, perfect calm... "twelve times ten is 120; twelve times eleven is 132; twelve times twelve is 144..." then over again, "...one times one is one; one times two is two..."

The river rushed and raged below, the bus teetered in its delicate balance, but Angie kept on, repeating over and over again the times tables—nothing else mattered, just the numbers...just the numbers....

With a violent lurch, the huge transport tow truck pulled the bus back onto the bridge. The high school principal had rushed to the scene. He had watched, helpless, as his students hung on the edge of death. He was there to wait in anguish for the arrival of the tow truck. When, after an eternity, it did arrive, he had watched the cables being attached, oh so carefully, oh so gently. He had seen the police cars turning back traffic at each end of the bridge; had seen the arrival of the emergency rescue team and ambulances. Scuba divers had been sent to the river's edge, waiting, ages ago. He had stared at the gently swaying bus with its load of silent, motionless young people; he had stared and wondered at their unbelievable calm.

The jolt of the two front wheels hitting solid ground broke the spell. A wild, chaotic cheer went up both from inside and outside the bus. The principal was the first to board, forcing open the twisted doors and crunching up the glass-covered steps two at a time.

"Well," he said to the driver, clasping him round the shoulders in a giant bear hug, "Congratulations to you, sir!" His voice choked in relief. "You have done a wonderful thing here. But, how did you keep it so calm? How did you do it?"

"Oh, it wasn't me," said the driver with a pale smile, pointing back down the aisle with a still-shaking hand, "It wasn't me. It was that blonde girl there, the one with the blue jacket on."

The principal turned and looked her way. "And what's your name, young lady? It seems we all owe an awful lot to you."

When the cheering and whistling and clapping had died down, she looked him straight in the eye; somehow she knew that things were going to be different.

"Angie, sir," she said. "My name is Angie."

The Year That Chanukah Came In the Middle of Summer

ISAAC BASHEVIS SINGER

There was talk about the belief that Chanukah* is only half a holiday and Aunt Yentl said: "To some it is only half a holiday, to others it is less than half. But to children Chanukah is the most beautiful of all holidays: the Chanukah lights on the windowsill, the gifts the youngsters receive, the potato pancakes, the games of dreidel*! The boys go to heder (school) only half a day, the girls practise dancing. Many weddings were celebrated on Chanukah. In our town it was the custom that children built a snowman on the eighth day of Chanukah—with two dried prunes for eyes and an old stocking cap on his head. As a rule the heder boys and girls did not mix, but when it came to playing dreidel and building the snowman, they played together.

"As I talk about it," Aunt Yentl continued, "a strange story comes to mind. It happened at least some seventy years ago and maybe even seventy-five years back. I was still a little girl then, and I loved Chanukah more than any other time in the year.

"Behind our town there was an estate that belonged to a rich man named Reb* Falik. He and his wife Malka had five children—four boys and one girl, Teibele, the youngest. When there are four boys and only one girl in a family she is treated like a princess. Teibele's parents were crazy about her.

"It was not the custom to send a girl to heder, but her father sent Teibele to heder to study like a boy. She was showered with toys. I still remember that one of her dolls was almost as large as Teibele herself. The real Teibele was no less beautiful than her fancy doll, perhaps even more so.

"One day the news spread that Teibele was dangerously ill. An abscess had developed in her throat and it became so big that she could hardly swallow her food. Needless to say, her parents tried their best to save her. They brought great doctors from Lublin* and even from as far away as Warsaw*. Nowadays, doctors can operate in such cases, but in those days they did not know what to do. The doctors prescribed medicine for Teibele, but to no avail. They applied leeches, cups and other old-fashioned remedies without results. Teiebele's mother Malka traveled to saintly rabbis asking that they pray for her child's recovery. Heder boys recited psalms in the synagogue for her. But her condition worsened every day. People began to say that the child was doomed. But for what sins? Reb Falik and Malka were both God-fearing and charitable people. Teibele herself had a heart of gold. She used to give all her toys to poor children.

"Teibele was a clever child for her seven years and she understood what was coming. She could not swallow solid food anymore and even drinking some tea became increasingly difficult. She lost a lot of weight and became emaciated. In those times Jews seldom kept dogs, but Reb Falik and Malka had a dog. His name was Charny, which in Polish means 'black.' Teibele loved Charny and Charny loved Teibele. Since she had gotten sick the dog sat all the time at her bed and kept watch on her, his shiny eyes seeming to say: I know you suffer and I love you.

"Once when her parents sat at Teibele's bedside trying to comfort her, Teibele said: 'I know that God wants me to die and I am not afraid anymore. But I wish to live until the end of Chanukah, with all the fun of playing dreidel, the snowman, the gifts and the rest of it.' Reb Falik and Malka promised the girl that she would go on living for a long time. But they knew that it was far too late for Teibele to reach Chanukah.

"It was only the middle of summer and the doctors had given her just a few weeks to live. Teibele's parents heard her say: 'Why must Chanukah be always in the winter? Why couldn't it be in the summer?'

"The moment Teibele said these words the grief-stricken father knew what to do. He decided to make a Chanukah celebration right then and there, even if he had to spend his whole fortune.

"First they went to the rabbi and asked whether it was allowed to celebrate Chanukah in the summer. The rabbi's verdict was that the pleasure of the sick child is more important than a date on the calendar.

"Reb Falik had many servants and friends, and they all loved Teibele. They energetically began to prepare the celebration. Reb Falik's bookkeeper was also an avid reader, and he told the people that in some countries on the other side of the equator Chanukah is celebrated in the summer.

"The next evening all was ready: the silver Chanukah lamp with its eight candles, the potato pancakes, the dreidels, the gifts for the children, not only for this family but also for many children in the town. The only problem was the snowman. How does one make a snowman in summer?

"But tailors and seamstresses found a way. They sewed a large white sack resembling the figure of a man with arms and legs and a head, and they stuffed it with down. Reb Falik blessed the Chanukah candles—without pronouncing God's name—and distributed the gifts to the children.

"Of course, the most beautiful gift was for Teibele. Then Malka and her maids brought in the tea and hot potato pancakes sprinkled with sugar and cinnamon and everyone enjoyed the repast. Although Teibele could not swallow, she bit off a piece, chewed it and said that it tasted delicious.

"Then the children began to play dreidel. Teibele's hand was too weak to make the dreidel spin, and her mother helped her. She won a lot that night and her eyes beamed with joy. At the appointed moment the two older boys brought in the snowman.

"All this time the dog Charny had been sitting quietly. He was treated to leftover pancakes, which he swallowed ravenously. But at the moment he saw the snowman, he began to bark and howl in the most violent way. Then he threw himself on the strange figure and tore it to pieces. The down fell out and spread over the room, just like snow. A great commotion arose among the children and the adults as well. Everybody's hair turned white with down. Reb Falik's black beard became snow-white. From wallowing in the feathers, Charny became a white dog.

"When Teibele saw the black dog turned white, she burst out laughing and could not stop. It was the first time in many weeks that she had been able to laugh, and so intense was her laughter that her abscess burst. Blood poured from her mouth, and in a minute the child was cured.

"A great miracle had happened on that summer night. Half the town came running, men, women, children. The town doctor came to witness the wondrous event. So did the rabbi and the priest. Some people laughed, others cried from joy and praised God for His mercy.

"When Reb Falik came to himself after the miracle that happened to his daughter, he announced that from now on he would celebrate Chanukah twice a year: once in the winter and once in the summer on the day when Teibele was cured. He promised big donations to the sick and the poor and various other charities.

"As to Teibele, she asked her parents' permission to change the dog's name from Charny to Bialy, the Polish word for white. And this remained his name. He got many gifts besides: a new doghouse with a little carpet and the juiciest bones.

"Of course, the animal could not understand why the family changed his name and lavished so much love on him, but God gives to every creature just as much understanding as it needs for its existence. So it is written in the Holy Books." And with that, Aunt Yentl finished her story.

---

* **Chanukah** (pronounced HAH·nuh·kuh): the festival of lights, celebrating the Jews' reclamation of their temple from the Greeks. It usually occurs in December.

* **dreidel:** a toy similar to a spinning top

* **Reb:** a Yiddish term of respect, similar to sir or mister

* **Lublin:** city in southeastern Poland

* **Warsaw:** capital of Poland

The Third Moon Of Tagor

LOUISE HAWES

After Mr. Litchum, our ninth-grade PE teacher, shows us movies about sex, he always turns off the projector, folds his arms and says, "Well, guys, that about covers it. Any questions?" Of course, he asks it like if anyone has questions after such a great film, they must be a pervert. So nobody ever asks anything.

The girls watch the same movie in another room with the school nurse. Even though Ms. McNally can take a joke and is a lot nicer than Litchum, I'll bet nobody asks her questions, either. I mean, those diagrams of reproductive organs and those scenes in the back seat of a car where a girl with big, sad eyes tells a dork who's pawing her she doesn't want to go "all the way," are okay. They just don't have much to do with being fifteen, never having been on a date in your life, and falling in love with Linda Spinelli's neck.

Sure, I would have liked to talk to someone when everything started getting crazy this semester. But even if Litchum was the friendly type, I don't think he could have helped much. An army couldn't have stopped me from staring at Linda's neck during math class, from spending the whole marking period studying the fine, short hair that grew all fuzzy and soft until it was long enough to get scooped into her pony tail. The A-Team*,

Rambo* and Conan the Barbarian* couldn't have made me concentrate on square roots instead of the dividing line where her white scoop-necked blouses stopped and Linda started.

So there I was, sports fans. Helpless, confused and failing math. Now don't get me wrong. Mark Wideman is no weirdo. I paid attention to those movies and I know all the facts. It's just that no one told me I was going to get a crush on this really popular girl I couldn't even talk to. Linda is a JV cheerleader plus she's got this round face like a little kid's and these monster brown eyes that make your mouth get dry every time you look at her.

Linda sits three seats over and one up from me in math. So whenever she scroonched down over a test or took her cardigan off because the room got too hot, I'd get blinded by that long, white neck. Maybe not blinded, but I'd keep seeing the round bump of her top vertebrae and those soft little hairs kind of superimposed over stuff for a while. Like when you stare at a light bulb until it gets burned into your eyeballs and you see it even after you've turned away. Most of the time, I never even heard the bell ring at the end of class.

The way I look at it, I wasn't really in love with Linda's neck. I was just being realistic. Except for a bunch of freckles on her nose and arms, Linda is about the cutest girl in the universe. And, even though my grandfather used to call me "Mark the Magnificent," I'm not exactly what you'd call big screen material. I'm sort of skinny, I drink milk with lunch and I bat sixteenth on the softball team. Linda's neck was the most I could hope for.

Until I got a story in *Thunder Hall*. *Thunder Hall* is our literary magazine and the editor is a gorp named Susan Daveen who runs around in day-glo tights and whispers instead of talks. Susan came running up to me last week when I was on line in the cafeteria. "I really adored your story, Mark," she whispered. It sounded like she'd just run a marathon the way she was panting. "It was deeply moving. I never knew you were so sensitive."

"And *I* didn't know Kelso was passing around my story," I said. "I told him I didn't want to submit it." Mr. Kelso is my English teacher and when I handed in this story about my grandfather dying, he got all runny and said how great it would be if I'd share my feelings with other kids who might have lost someone they cared about, too. I said I didn't think grandfathers were dropping like flies and that, even if they were, I didn't want my story in the dorkiest magazine since *Humpty Dumpty**. Which shows you how much good it does to tell a teacher anything.

I tried to stay home the day "In Memorium" came out. My mistake was telling Mom I had a headache, stomach pains and a sore throat. I think if I'd left out the sore throat, she wouldn't have shined a flashlight in my mouth, taken my temperature and asked to check my homework. I wore my black sweat shirt and black cords. I figured if I was going to be humiliated, I might as well dress for it. After lunch, when the monitors handed out copies of *Thunder Hall*, I really *did* get a headache and stomach pains. By the time Math class rolled around, the sore throat part of the program was starting. I was just about to raise my hand to go to the nurse when Linda Spinelli leaned back in her desk and smiled right at me.

She was leaning so far back that the neckline of her blouse was stretched really wide. What I mostly saw was the pale, shiny skin along her collar bone; what I sort of saw out of the corner of my eye was that she was passing me a note. "I really loved your story," she'd written. "I didn't know you were so sencitive!" There was a heart instead of a dot at the bottom of the exclamation mark. I was pretty sure that if someone like Susan Daveen had written the note, there wouldn't be a *c* in *sensitive*. But I also knew that if Dippy Daveen had written me, I wouldn't be getting all sweaty and feeling like every muscle in my body had turned into mashed potatoes!

My brain froze solid, sports fans. I just sat there with this sappy smile on my face and the note in my hand. I knew Linda wanted me to answer her in the space she'd left under "write back." It was about half the page, but it might as well have been a whole legal pad! I couldn't think of anything to say—except, "I like your neck," which would have been hard to write with paralyzed fingers!

The whole ninth grade had to take a half-period course this year called "Creative Thinking." I guess it paid off, because I suddenly realized I didn't have to choose between hurting Linda's feelings by not answering her note and dragging my claw hand across the page in a baby scrawl she wouldn't be able to read anyway. What I did was take a pencil and *pretend* to start writing.

I licked the tip of the pencil, I scratched my head, I even winked at Linda like I had something really terrific to say. Then, I moved my hand over the page, back and forth, up and down, like I was writing up a storm. In between lines, I looked up at Linda. She was giggling and punching elbows with Tracy

Stedman. You could tell she was pretty excited at all the trouble I was going to.

Then, just as I was on the fourth line, I pushed as hard as I could on the pencil. I mean pushed. I kept my other hand in front of my writing hand, so it looked like I was afraid someone might see all the gooshy, swoony stuff I was pouring out. Actually, I didn't want Linda to see my knuckles turning white from how hard I was bearing down on that number two! CRACK! It buckled and shot into space like a fire cracker. The whole class, including Mr. Ferrante, our math teacher who was writing problems on the board, turned around.

Mr. Ferrante is skinny like me, but a lot taller and he wears glasses. If you wave to him in the cafeteria, he never waves back. At first, I though he was a real snob, then I figured out he can't see more than three feet in front of him! So when my pencil-rocket took off, he just stood there with his all-purpose tough look on his face and asked, "What's going on, boys?" (He got the boys part right, but since the girls in the class hardly ever do stuff, the odds were in his favor.)

I just raised both hands in the air and made a goofy face. Linda passed a pencil to Tracy who passed it to Doug Raymond who passed it to me. Mr. Ferrante turned back to the board, everything quieted down and I started "writing" again. This time, I got to the third line before I pressed on the pencil with every ounce of mashed-potato muscle I had. Sure enough, another CRACK! and the pencil somersaulted over Billy Hanover's head. There were only six minutes left in the period. I figured unless Linda passed me a ballpoint, I had it made.

When the third pencil broke, I looked real angry and tore up the note. I take that back about the big screen. I may not have movie star looks, but I sure can act! Linda had this real neat pout on her face when she came up to me after class. "Why'd you tear it up?" she asked, her lips all pink and shiny. "If you grow up to be a famous author, that note could be worth a fortune."

I just smiled. That's because my brain was still frozen. Normally, sports fans, I'm no motor mouth, but I can carry on a conversation. Not with Linda's lips and legs and sweater and all her other parts together right in front of me! It was like Linda was on TV and I was watching her. It never even entered my mind that I could actually talk back! She stood there a few more minutes, looking pretty and confused, then said, "See ya," and walked away. I went straight home and talked to my mirror.

It was much easier with the mirror than it had been with Linda. I thought of all kinds of snappy openers like, "How's it going?" and "What's up?" I practised till they were automatic, till I had just the right combination of friendliness and coolness in my voice. Before bed, I picked out a beige sweater and a brown and green-striped shirt for the next day. (Every time I wear that shirt, my mother gets this soupy look and kisses me behind my left ear, so I know it looks good.)

I woke up dreaming about my grandfather. He was yelling at grandma about all the pills he was supposed to take after he got sick. "Edith," he roared just the way he used to, "if God or Mother Nature or anyone else with our best interest at heart intended us to solve all our problems with pills, they certainly wouldn't put them in a bottle and charge us $50.95 for thirty."

I guess the dream was still in my head at breakfast. Mom always puts a vitamin C by my orange juice and that morning, I just left it there. Mom didn't care; she was too busy looking at my outfit. "Your math may be taking a nose-dive," she said, "but you've finally learned to match colors." With all that time I'd put in front of the mirror, it was only natural I'd be dressed a little better than usual. But Mom had this something-is-up-and-I-bet-I-know-what-it-is smile on her face. It was the sort of smile where even if the person *does* know what's up, you sure don't want to encourage them.

"Ninth grade is no time to dress like a geek," I told her. "Harley Ellis wore a pair of velcro sneakers to school yesterday. The guys have already nicknamed him *Blue Light Special.*"

The part about Harley's sneaks was true. It was just that it happened a lot earlier in the year, that's all. I suppose if you added up all my half-lies, you'd come up with a lot of whole ones, but it doesn't bother me that way. Besides, I'm not sure Mom would have believed me if I told her about Linda. Whenever she talks to me or my sister about sex, she always starts out by saying things like, "When you get older," or "It might be hard to understand now."

When I walked out of my Friday science lab, I walked into Linda. She was with her best friend and shadow, Marcy Havens. I hadn't practiced talking to *two* girls, but still I felt pretty cool. "What's up, Minda?" I asked in my Tom Cruise voice. "How's it going, Larcy?" I couldn't believe it was me talking. What a jerk, I thought. How could anybody be so dumb? I just stood there, my backpack slung real casual over one shoulder, and listened to this complete nerd blow himself away in front of two of the cutest girls in George Washington High!

But Linda didn't even notice. She shoved this copy of *Thunder Hall* at me. "Would you autograph your story for me, Mark?" She was wearing a yellow sleeveless blouse and there was a blue, fuzzy sweater tied around her waist, its arms hugging her. She handed me a pen and she and Marcy stood there, waiting. I bent my head over the story, trying not to look at Linda's blouse, trying to remember my name. It came to me, sports fans, and I handed the pen and the magazine back to her.

Linda looked disappointed. "Just your name?" she said.

"I thought that's what an autograph was," I told her, confused. Just before her blouse disappeared under her sweater, it pulled real tight. She smelled clean and new, sort of like just-washed socks.

"I thought you'd say something like, 'To my friend Linda. I'll always remember.' Something like that."

I wanted to nuzzle her neck but I smiled like Johnny Dep instead. "That's year-book stuff," I said. You rate more than that."

I had bought myself time, but not much. Linda looked at Marcy, who shrugged and turned to me. Then Linda did one of her great pouts and zapped me with her laser eyes. She was wearing her hair in a pony tail pulled to one side and she started loosening the rubber band around it. "Like what?" she asked. I didn't have the faintest idea. But it wouldn't have made much more sense to admit that than it would have to bury my face in the soft place right under her chin. Which I was straining most of my stomach muscles to keep from doing. It's crazy, sports fans, but all the time we were talking about writing I was thinking about tasting her skin. I wondered if it would be all salty and sweet like my sister's when she was a baby. I know. I know. I'm definitely a pervert.

"What do I rate, Mark?" She had loosened her hair and let it fall all around her face. She rolled up the magazine and used it like a megaphone. "Hey, Mark Wideman. Planet Earth to Mark. Come in!"

Marcy was giggling and trying not to at the same time. It sounded like somebody was choking a chicken. At least like when they choke a chicken in cartoons. Only I didn't see what was so funny.

"A story, of course." It came out of my mouth, sports fans, but I swear it didn't visit my brain first. It was like somebody else had said it. Linda and I were both surprised.

"A story?" She looked really happy, like I was throwing her a party or something. "A story just for me?"

"Sure." Great. I was thoroughly crazy. I was doomed. "It's all about you and it's almost finished."

"OOOOOH!" Linda hugged the magazine to her chest and squealed. I was dead meat. I was also absent from school for three days this week.

I thought I could finish the story over the weekend. But writing about Linda was a lot harder than writing about my grandfather. And not just because he's dead and she isn't. The truth is, I know a lot of stuff about grandpa. Like the way he knew he was dying even though everyone pretended he wasn't. (Once in the hospital, when my grandmother and aunt were talking about things like fixing the garage door and the price of Brussels sprouts, he looked over at me and smiled. It was really weird, because even though he didn't say anything, I understood that he understood that Brussels sprouts made them feel safe and normal.)

I know what grandpa liked: going to baseball games with me, making things out of scraps of used lumber and old bicycle parts, listening to my dumb sister play "Some Enchanted Evening" over and over on the piano, and yelling at my grandmother. And I know what he didn't like: taking pills, talking about politics with my mother, and cleaning the roof gutters every spring.

But what did I know about Linda? Besides what I'd been studying in math, of course. Sure, she was great to look at and she gave out this electricity that short-circuited my brain every time she got near me. But what did she like to do when she was alone? Did she lock her bedroom door and listen to Billy Joel* like my sister? Did she read science fiction like me?

When she got angry, did she yell like Grandpa or do a slow burn like my mother? What made her laugh? Did she like animals? Would she have picked up my mouse, Herman, if he hadn't gotten lost when he gnawed his way out of the wooden fun house I built for him? Did she always do her homework? Did she think some of the football cheers were pretty moronic?

I knew zilch about my dream girl, sports fans. And that would make pretty poor reading. After two days of living in the library and filling the waste basket in the next-to-last study carrel with wadded up paragraphs that got nowhere, I decided I needed a fresh approach. Well, not exactly fresh, but different. So on Monday, I left for school like usual, but went back to the library instead. I started leafing through the books in the J through L stack. It was right beside my carrel, and I figured it was as good a place to start as any.

I looked for stories about women or girls. I found this neat book by someone named P.D. James*. It was all about a lady detective named Cordelia Gray. I got really interested in this whole house full of people (including a murderer) before I realized Cordelia wasn't much like Linda. At least as far as I knew.

I don't usually read poetry, but the inside flap of a long poem called *Cawdor* by this guy, Robinson Jeffers*, said it was a story "full of the torment and passion of Phaedra*, the greatest of tragic heroines." I didn't find much about heroines, but there was this part where the poem talks about an eagle locked in a cage. I don't know why, but I must have read it ten times — it had nothing to do with Linda, but it was sad and beautiful and angry all at the same time.

I was sure it was about a girl, so I started reading this book called *Kim* even though it was pretty long. Of course, Kim wasn't a girl; he was a little boy who became sort of a spy in India. Kipling* is almost as good a writer as P.D. James, so I wasted some more time. The problem is, when I like something I read it real slow, like I don't want to miss anything.

Yesterday, I was still in the *K*s. I was pretty sure the first book I picked wasn't going to be a big help, but it had such a great title, I had to take a look. *Oh Dad, Poor Dad, Mamma's Hung You in the Closet and I'm Feelin' So Sad* turned out to be a play written by this guy named Arthur Kopit*. The Dad in the play was dead, so he didn't have any lines, and the Mom bossed her kid around a lot. When I got to the part about the piranha and the Venus' flytraps*, I sort of hated to put the book back.

I took one of the *L* books home with me. I already told you I'm a science fiction freak and I spotted this terrific illustration of a dragon fighting a boy on the cover of *The Wizard of Earthsea* by Ursula K. Le Guin*. It's all about this kid who lives in a place that's mostly water and islands. The boy is studying to be a wizard and there aren't really any girls in the book at all. But once I start a good story like that, there's no way I'm going to stop!

It was close to the time school gets out, when I finally found the book I needed. It's by a lady named Lucy Linbeck and it was perfect. It's number 13 in a series called Hillsboro High and it's got a picture of a cheerleader on the front. I checked it out with *Earthsea* and took it home. I read both books in bed.

If the other books in the Hillsboro High series are like *Too Young To Stop*, regular readers must get pretty depressed. The story's about this cute cheerleader (who has blond hair in the book but who was going to have red hair like Linda in my story) and everything in the world happens to her. Her big sister gets pregnant, her father has a heart attack, her boyfriend breaks up with her and someone steals the prom fund that her cheerleading squad has spent all semester collecting.

Not that I'd copy anybody's story exactly. I decided right away I would stick in the cheerleader's best friend, Marcy, and her brother. (I found out from Wallace Newsolm who's a good friend of Robby Furlowe who likes Janet Silverman who lives next door to Marcy that Linda has a big brother named Jason.) So now Jason was going to get his girlfriend pregnant and, of course, Hillsboro High would be George Washington High. Then, after Linda found out the prom fund was missing, she'd ask me, instead of her ex-boyfriend, to help find out who took it.

"What on earth are you reading?" My Mom looked really surprised when she caught me reading *Too Young To Stop* last night. But then she got her know-it-all smile, with these tender, crinkly eyes. She sat down on my bed. "Did you take that from your sister's room?"

It was a lot better to have Mom think I was a sneak than to have to explain about Linda and *Thunder Hall* and my big foot in my even bigger mouth. It was another one of those half-lies that go down easy. "I know this book is really for girls, Mom." I smiled, too, now and sat up next to her, closing the book. "But it's a pretty good story."

Behind the cheerleader on the cover was a football field and one guy was running for a touchdown with about six players after him. "You know," Mom told me, "your sister and I had a long talk about these books before she started reading them."

I figured the guy with the ball was the cheerleader's boyfriend, even though she wasn't looking at the game. "Don't worry," I said. "There isn't any kissing until the last page."

"Sometimes I wish your father lived closer." I sort of knew what Mom meant, even though she was the one who had asked for the divorce.

"Hey, we covered all that stuff with Mr. Litchum," I told her. My mother is kind of short and right then, sitting next to her, I felt like she was a little girl. I put my arm around her. "I'm cool."

She laughed and kissed me behind the left ear. Then she stood up. "Just get that book back to Hillary's room before she finds it's missing. She still hasn't forgotten about the eyebrow tweezers."

"I needed them for the decals on my shuttle model. It's not as if I ruined them or anything. I think they look better with the silver paint, anyway."

My mom just smiled again and shut the door real quietly, like she was an accessory to the crime of the century. I got back to cutie pie and number 13 and the case of the missing prom fund. It turned out that the class drip had stolen the money to help pay for an operation his crippled sister needed. Naturally, the whole class rolled up their sleeves, raised money all over town and helped the drip's sister walk again.

I decided to have the school janitor steal the money in my story. Mr. Sanchez is Mexican, I think. He has this little daughter who has big black eyes and sucks her thumb. Just before I fell asleep, I pictured this great final scene with Linda lifting Mr. Sanchez' daughter out of a hospital bed and teaching her to walk again. I didn't know if Linda liked to cry, but I hoped so.

I woke up this morning from another dream about Grandpa. He looked like he used to before he got sick. He was wearing one of the button-down sweaters he always liked and he was working on a weird machine in the basement. "Don't come any closer," he warned as I tried to figure out what all the wheels and gears and gizmos were for. Then he put the machine in the center of the floor and pushed a red button on one of its wheels.

You should have seen the way that invention or whatever it was worked! It sort of lit up all over with this thin green glow and the wheels and gears made a noise like singing. I can't tell you exactly why, but it seemed like the greatest, most magical thing in the world. "Wow!" I said when I saw the glow and heard the music. "What's it do?"

I guess I must have seemed pretty confused, because my grandfather looked at me and burst out laughing. Not the hoarse little hospital laugh he had at the end, but one of the big I-don't-give-a-darn-who-hears-me laughs he used to have. He looked at me, then he looked at his creation and then he looked at me again. All the time, he just kept laughing so hard I thought he'd hurt himself. I could still hear him laughing after I woke up and started writing Linda's story.

I worked on "Linda Saves the Day" for half an hour before I got dressed. Then I worked on it some more at the library. Once I got going, it went really fast. I was finished before lunch, so I decided to go to school late so I could give it to her today. You don't need a note for getting *into* school, only getting out, so Mr. Kelso just kind of nodded when I walked into the middle of his English class.

My seat is right next to Susan Daveen's since I got moved for talking to Tad Worth while Mr. Kelso was explaining paragraph structure. I hid "Linda Saves the Day" inside my binder. I put *Too Young to Stop* and *The Wizard of Earthsea* (which I was going to return to the library on the way home) on top of my desk. Susan spotted them right away.

"Did you like that story?" she asked, uncrossing her pink tights and leaning real close.

"Not really," I told her. Mr. Kelso had fallen in love with listening to himself and he wasn't even looking in our direction. "The plot was pretty dumb and I wouldn't have cared if all the characters dropped off a steep cliff."

Susan looked shocked. "How can you say that?" Her whispery voice had turned loud and indignant. I was afraid Kelso would hear her, but he was still wrapped up in trying to tell us why nobody ever made a movie of *The Catcher in the Rye**. "She's one of the best writers I've ever read!" Susan's eyes were all wet at the edges like she was going to cry or something.

"Okay, okay." I said. "I guess she's all right if you like soap operas and stuff. I just mean I wish she'd write about important things."

Susan didn't look like she was going to cry anymore. She looked more like she was going to explode. "Ursula K. Le Guin never wrote about anything unimportant in her whole life!" she yelled.

"Ursula K. Le Guin!" Boy did I feel ridiculous. "I thought you were talking about Lucy Linbeck."

"Who?"

"Lucy Linbeck. You know. Hillsboro High." I held up

number 13. Susan stuck a finger down her throat and made a gagging noise. "

You *read* that junk?" she asked.

I almost wished Kelso would snap out of it and catch us. I felt really dumb. "Of course not," I told her. "It's my sister's. I just thought you..."

"You just thought I what?"

"Well, you're a girl and I figured..." Susan was wearing a turtle neck, so I couldn't see if her neck was long and white like Linda's. "Have you read *Wizard of Earthsea*?"

"Of course." Susan stopped looking sad. She stopped looked angry. This kind of blush started creeping up from the edge of her turtleneck all the way to her forehead. She looked as excited as a little kid at Christmas. "I've read all her books. Didn't you love the part where Ged casts a spell and lets the shadow loose?"

"I sure did," I said. "And what about where he finds out its name? That was really neat!"

Guess what, sports fans? It turns out Dippy Daveen isn't so dippy after all. In fact, she's read most of the same books I have and she's really into science fiction! Even after the bell cut Kelso off and he let us go, Susan and I couldn't stop talking. She told me about this really neat series by a guy named Piers Anthony* and I told her about this story I made up called "The Third Moon of Tagor."

It's about this faraway planet called Tagor where people have eyes on both sides of their heads and they never die. There are three giant moons that circle Tagor; it's always bright because two of the moons orbit one way and the third moon orbits the other way. The Tagorians like it that way, but of course they've never known night. (They sleep in long chains, eye to eye, so the moonlight doesn't keep them awake. The chains always form a circle, the Tagorians eyeballing each other in the center and their hairy legs fanning out like rays.)

Susan really liked my story and she had this terrific idea for an ending where some villains who try to destroy the third moon of Tagor are defeated by a mind-meld when all the Tagorians join forces with a race of small, rabbit-like creatures that inhabit the moons. We stood there in the hall after English, talking like we'd known each other since kindergarten. It was weird, the way I felt then.

It wasn't like talking to Linda at all. I didn't get the

shakes or even break into a sweat. It was easy and natural, just like talking to a guy. Only better. Susan's skinnier that Linda, but I decided she's kind of cute. She's got pale, faraway blue eyes, plus this scratchy little laugh in her throat when she gets excited. It sort of tickled my ears. It wasn't like Grandpa's laugh, but it gave me the same good feeling.

We talked so long I was late to math class. When I walked in, I could tell Linda was glad to see me. She nudged Marcy, then turned around and zapped a giant smile at me. It was pretty neat, because about half the kids in class saw it.

I made a big deal out of wrestling "Linda Saves the Day" from the middle of my binder and passing it up to Linda. The funny thing is, though, I stopped thinking about Linda while Mr. Ferrante was teaching. Not that I had any idea what he was talking about while he jabbed stubby pieces of chalk into the blackboard and waved his hands in the air like he was conducting music. I was too busy thinking about Susan!

All through math, right up until the bell rang, I was planning how Susan and I would finish "Third Moon of Tagor" together. I also thought a lot about the way her blue turtle neck hid her neck and the way her eyes got all misty and dreamy when she talked about stuff she liked. I was still thinking about Susan when Linda rushed up to my desk after class.

"Oh, Mark," she said "I can't believe you wrote this just for me!" She held the seven pages I'd written tight against her chest. "This is absolutely the most awesome story that's ever been written!"

"Even counting *Catcher in the Rye*?" I was only kidding, but Linda didn't get the joke. She stopped beaming and hugged the story tighter.

"Actually, I haven't read *Catcher*. I wanted to, but Mr. Kelso picked the wrong semester to assign it. I mean, its's football season and I've got practice *every* day!" She was finished feeling guilty, I guess, because she gave me another of her laser smiles. "I thought the Cliff notes were pretty good, though."

"Well, I'm glad you liked my story." It had been so easy to think up stuff to talk to Susan about, but I'd already run dry with Linda. "I'm writing another one."

Linda smiled again. It was like she had only one expression. I wondered if I told her my dog was dead, if she'd still flash those white teeth of hers. Maybe she couldn't help it, maybe her smile was on automatic.

"That's great," she said. "What's your new story about?"

I told her about Tagor and all its moons. I told her about the galactic invasion and the way the Tagorians were going to have to overcome their enemy to save themselves. You guessed it, sports fans. She smiled. "That's nice," she told me. "But why don't you write another one about GW High? I could read that kind of story forever!"

"Yeah," I said. "The only problem is I couldn't go on *writing* them forever. They're sort of boring."

At least Linda stopped smiling. She looked like I'd said something bad about babies or mothers or something. I thought about sticking my finger down my throat and making Susan's gagging noise, but I just said goodbye instead.

My ex-dream girl stood there with her mouth open, and I raced off down the hall. I was already late. I'd promised Susan I would meet her after school so we could start on the first chapter of "The Third Moon of Tagor."

* **The A-Team:** television show popular in the 1980s
* **Rambo:** character played by Sylvester Stallone in a series of films made in the 1980s
* **Conan the Barbarian:** character in a 1981 film starring Arnold Schwarzenegger
* *Humpty Dumpty*: a magazine for children aged four to six.
* **Billy Joel:** a classically trained pianist; he became a popular singer-songwriter in the 1970s and 1980s
* **P.D. James** (pseudonym of Phyllis Dorothy White): British writer of mystery, crime, and suspense novels
* **Robinson Jeffers:** American poet noted for his long narrative poems.
* **Phaedra:** A Greek legend in which Phaedra loved Hippolytus, her son-in-law. When he rejected her, she wrote a vengeful letter lying about Hippolytus and then hanged herself.
* **Rudyard Kipling:** late 19th century-early 20th century British writer born in India
* **Arthur Kopit:** American playwright and director
* **Venus' flytrap:** an insect-eating plant
* **Ursula K. Le Guin:** popular writer of short stories, poetry and novels, most of which are science fiction or fantasy. See "Darkness Box."
* *The Catcher in the Rye*: award-winning novel by American writer J.D. Salinger
* **Piers Anthony** (pseudonym of Anthony D. Jacob): popular American writer of numerous science fiction and fantasy novels

Who Said We All Have to Talk Alike

WILMA ELIZABETH MCDANIEL

Who knows how Neffie Pike's speech pattern was formed? Her Ozark* family had talked the same way for generations. They added an "r" to many words that did not contain that letter. In spite of this, or because of it, their speech was clear and colorful and to the point. Most people understood what they were talking about, exactly.

Neffie was her parents' daughter. She called a toilet, "torelet," and a woman, "worman," very comfortably. The teacher at the country school never attempted to change Neffie's manner of speaking. She said that Neffie had a fine imagination and should never allow anyone to squelch it. In fact, Neffie never really knew that she talked different from most other people.

People in the tiny community of Snowball really loved Neffie. She was a good neighbor, unfailingly cheerful and helpful. The appearance of her tall and bony figure at the door of a sickroom or a bereaved family meant comfort and succor. A great woman, everyone in Snowball agreed.

She would have probably lived her life out in the same lumber house if her husband had not died. In the months that followed his death, she developed a restless feeling. Home chores, church and charity work did not seem to be enough to occupy her mind. She started to read big-town newspapers at the library in nearby Marshall, something new for her. She became especially interested in the out-of-state employment want ads. She mentioned to neighbors, "They are a lot of good jobs out there in the world."

One day she came home from Marshall and stopped at old Grandma Meade's house. She sat down in a canebottom chair and announced, "I have got me a job in California. I am a selling my house and lot to a couple of retired people from Little Rock. They will be moving in the first of June."

Grandma Meade sat in shocked silence for several seconds, then said, "Honey, I do not believe it. I mean that I never in the world imagined that you would consider leaving Snowball. You and Lollis was so happy together here." Her voice trailed off, "Of course nobody could foretell the Lord would call him so young."

Neffie looked stonily at her and said with her usual clarity, "A widder woman is a free woman, especially if she don't have no children. She ought to be free to come and go like she pleases. After all, I am only fifty-one years old. I can do as much work as I ever did. This job is taking care of two little girls while their mother works at some high-paying job. She has already sent me a bus ticket. I would be a fool not to go. Everyone has been to California except me. I always hankered to see the state for myself. Now is my chance to see some of the rest of the world. It may sound foolish, but it will sort of be like having a dorter of my own and grandchildren. I aim to write you a long letter when I get settled down out there."

Neffie left for California on schedule. After two weeks, Grandma Meade began to worry a bit. She said, "I thought that Neffie surely would have dropped us a line by now. The last thing she told me was that she would write me a long letter. Well, maybe she hasn't got settled down yet."

A month passed without any word from Neffie.

Bug Harrison was at Grandma Meade's house when Neffie returned the day after Snowball's big Fourth of July celebration.

Neffie put her suitcases down and began at the beginning. "Grandma, you was so right about so many things. I knowed I was in trouble hock-deep, only one minute after I stepped off that bus in California. A purty young worman came forward to meet me and said she was Beryl. I busted out and told her, 'My, you are a purty worman, even purtier than your pitcher.' She kinda shrunk back and looked at me like I had used a cussword. She stood there holding her little girls' hands and asked me, where on earth did you hear a word like worman, was it a female worm of some kind? She said, 'Worman is woe-man,' like you say woh to a horse.

"Her remark nearly knocked me off my feet. I felt like a fool, and I didn't even know why. My stomach started churning. I durst not say anything to defend myself, because I hadn't done anything wrong.

"We started to walk to Beryl's station wagon in the parking lot. I told her that I never was blessed with a dorter or son, either. That set her off again. She said that her children were at a very impressionable age, that I would have to watch my speech and learn the correct pronunciation of words. She did not want them picking up incorrect speech patterns and something she called coll-oke-ism, something I had, and didn't even realize. I decided to shut up and get in the car. The worman had already paid for my fare. I felt that I had to at least give her a few months' service, if I could stand the punishment at all.

"On our way to Beryl's house, she stopped at a drive-in restaurant and ordered cheeseburgers and milkshakes for all of us. I decided to just eat and listen.

"It was sure a pleasurable drive on to Beryl's home. We followed the same county highway for the entire seven miles. The road was lined on both sides with pams, tall with them fronds waving in the breeze. It reminded me of pitchers I have seen of The Holy Land*, really touched my heart. I forgot myself again and said that I never had seen pams before except in pitchers. Quick as a flash Beryl told me, 'They are pall-ms, not pams. There is an l in the word.' After that, I sure buttoned up my mouth. I just said yes or no to anything she asked me.

"Her house turned out to be a real nice place, bright and modern with every type of electrical gadget you could think of. There were four bedrooms, each with a bath. I was so tired and upset over Beryl's attitude that I begged off sitting up to visit with her and the little girls. I ran me a full tub of warm water and took me a long soaking bath. I fell into bed and went sound asleep. Worman, I plumb died away, slept all night without waking up. To show you how hard I slept, there was a fairly severe earthquake in the central part of California where Beryl lived. It even shook a few things off a living-room shelf. I tell you, I wouldn't have heard Gabriel* blow his horn that night.

"I woke up feeling relieved that it was Monday. Beryl left for work promptly at seven-thirty. That meant the girls and I had the house to ourselves. Worman, I am telling you, they was two living dolls, Pat and Penny. I made them bran muffins for breakfast and scrambled some eggs. They ate until they nearly foundered. It seemed like they had never seen a bran muffin before, asked me if I would cook them the same thing each day.

"I told them I knew how to cook other good old homely dishes, too. Every day, I tried something new on them, biscuits and sausage and milk gravy, buttermilk pancakes, waffles, popovers, French toast, corn dodgers, fried mush. You name it, worman, I cooked it for those dolls. It wouldn't be no big deal for the kids here in Snowball, they was raised to eat like that, but it was hog heaven to Pat and Penny."

Grandma Meade had been listening intently, her eyes pinned on Neffie's face. Now she asked, "How did Beryl like your cooking?"

Neffie laughed heartily. She said, "To put it plain she *loved* it. I can say that she never found any flaw in my cooking, only made one complaint connected with it. I boirled her a fine big cabbage and hamhock dinner and made cornbread for our supper one evening. When we started to sit down at the table, I said that it was a nice change to have a boirled dinner now and then. That set her off like a firecracker. She said, 'That is boiled, not boirled.' I decided to let that snide remark pass. I saw she started dishing up the food—she lit in on it like a starving hound-dog. That showed what she thought of my cooking, didn't it? My cooking sure helped me get through them weeks as good as I did."

Bug Harrison broke in, "What were your duties during the day?"

Neffie said, "I was hired to take care of the two little girls. That is what I done. I cooked because people have to eat. I always have, always will. That didn't put no extra strain on me. The girls and I played the most of the day. They would sit on each arm of my chair and listen to me tell them about my life back in Arkansas. I didn't hold back nothing. I told them about haunted houses, ghosts, robbers, bank holdups, tornadoes, snakes, tarantulas, times when the river flooded and we had to float on a rooftop to save our lives. Lordy, worman, they just ate it up. They would listen to me with their eyes as big as saucers. I don't quite know why I done it, but I asked the girls not to tell their mother about my stories. They were as secretive as little private detectives until a week ago. They got so excited over one of my stories that they forgot themselves. I was busy in the kitchen putting some homemade noodles into a pot of chicken broth. I heard Pat tell her mother, 'Mom, back in Arkansas where Neffie used to live, they are wormans that can tell fortunes for people. They can look right through your face and tell if you are telling the truth or a lie. They can rub your warts with skunk oirl and say some words and all the warts will fall off, never ever come back.' I figured I was in bad trouble, but I kept on dropping the noodles into the broth. I was a hundred percent right about the trouble.

"Beryl blowed her stack. She marched right back to the kitchen with the girls at her heels. She stood in the door and said, 'I have been afraid of this very thing. Neffie, I just can't keep you on any longer.'

"At that point, Pat and Penny throwed themselves down on the floor and started bawling like two young calves. Pat sobbed out real angry-like, 'Yes, you *can* keep Neffie! She is the best storyteller in the whole world and the best cooker. If she goes home to Arkansas, we won't never have no more biscuits and sausage and gravy.' The tears began to run down her little face.

"Beryl stood there with her face like a flintrock. It looked like she wanted to be nice to me, but that her duty come first with her. She drawed in her breath and said, 'Neffie, you are as good and kind and honest as you can be, exceptional, but your speech is totally unacceptable. My children are at a very impressionable age. I have tried to overlook it, but they are definitely being influenced in the wrong direction. They say dorter and orter with regularity. This pattern must be eradicated immediately. I shall be happy to pay your travelling expenses home. You can look on this trip out West as my vacation gift to you.' I could see that her mind was made up and she wasn't going to change it.

"I did think to ask her if she had some other babysitter in mind. I didn't want to run out and leave her in a bind without one. She said there was a young girl from the college who wanted day work, so she could attend night classes. She thought that would work out great. I got her point. The college girl would be different from me, more to suit Beryl.

"Well, to shorten my story, she bought me a big box of real expensive chocolates and put me on the bus with my paid ticket, just like she had promised. She and the girls stood there beside the bus waiting for it to pull out. Penny looked up at me and blew me a kiss. I heard her say as plain as plain could be, 'Neffie, you are a sweet worman.' Then I saw Beryl put her hand over Penny's mouth. Right then, the bus pulled out of the depot and I lost sight of them.

"Worman, I done a lot of thinking as that bus rolled along the highway. I would eat a chocolate and think over my experience with Beryl. Things kind of cleared up in my mind, like having blinders taken off of my eyes. I saw I had really been ignorant of some things that other folks knowed. I didn't talk right to suit some of them, but that wasn't my fault. *I didn't know we was all supposed to talk the same way*. I thought people hadn't all talked the same since before God tore down their tower at Babel* and confused all their tongues. Folks all over the world have talked different ever since then. I guess some of them like Beryl want to go back to pre-Babel days. Anyway, it was sure an eye-opener to me, hurt me, too. Beryl just plain separated herself from me. It was like she took a sharp knife and cut a melon in half, and throwed away the half that was me. You know what you do with a piece of melon you don't want. You throw it with the rinds into the garbage can. Worman, who said that we all have to talk alike? Can anyone tell me that?"

* **Ozark:** of or relating to the sparsely populated Ozark Mountains region, situated mainly in Missouri but also in Arkansas and Oklahoma

* **The Holy Land:** Israel and parts of Jordan

* **Gabriel:** one of the seven archangels in the Bible

* **Tower of Babel:** a tower which was to have its top "in the heavens" (Genesis 11: 1-9); according to the Bible, God punished such presumption by confusing the speech of the builders so that they could not finish the tower; since that time, there have been many different ways of speaking

White Christmas

ELAINE DRIEDGER

Wishing it would snow so hard that we couldn't possibly go to Florida, I glare at the cold, dark window of Oma's* sagging kitchen and see nothing but the reflection of my own face poking out from the swaying backs of my aunts.

In all my thirteen years I have never experienced a Christmas day as miserable as this one.

I grip a plate between the folds of my dishtowel, squeaking hot wetness from the glaze patterned with apple blossoms and a net of cracks. I've watched that window all afternoon. Watching for snow. Waiting for Janet. Dreaming of Larry.

Five aunts and Oma bustle around me, grabbing dishes from the dish rack or thumping up the steps to the pantry with zwieback* and perishky* left over from the Christmas fesper.* Aunt Betty and Aunt Lizzy compare crimpolene* prices, and my mother at the sink explains the details of her new Jello recipe to Aunt Frieda. I don't think Aunt Frieda could care less about a Jello recipe.

I am the only cousin in this steaming, rattling kitchen. The younger cousins are upstairs, watching "The Grinch Who Stole Christmas" on the TV in the spare room. I've sat here all afternoon as each new wave of relatives sprayed in more little cousins who flaunted new toys or scrambled under the battered table to bump my legs or snatch zwieback and cookies from the plates set out in the long, narrow pantry. I've been here every Christmas I can remember. This year should have been different.

Oma and Opa's* house on Christmas day is always the same. The uncles and Opa sit in the front room and argue about Trudeau*, farm co-ops, and Aeltester* Nichol's latest sermon. The women are in the middle room near the kitchen, where they can keep their ears tuned to the racket and rustle of the kids. The older cousins have stopped coming. Even Janet hasn't shown up yet. She's only a year older than I am. Whatever she did today had to be more fun than sitting in a noisy farm kitchen overrun by little kids.

I turn from the window, pull the plate from my damp cloth, and push it onto the growing pile on the table. As I hoist a bowl, dull and heavy, from the dish rack, I scowl at my mother's back. There is no place for me here anymore. I'm in high school now. Janet hasn't come since she was in grade eight.

It should have been different this year. But my parents insisted on their way, saying that Uncle George should keep Janet more in line. I felt like screaming: How could I ever face Larry if he knew I was being treated like a kid?

I wince now remembering my father's teasing me in front of Oma and Aunt Frieda when we'd arrived this afternoon. My kid sister Karen hadn't said a thing, but I could see smirks all over her face.

"Linda is probably thinking about her boyfriend today, eh. Isn't that right? Real good-looking fellow. Drives a red convertible." My father's eye had winked like it was trying to catch me.

And it had. All day I've been caught—between the tinsel-sparkling, light-bubbling Christmas tree and the cool gleam of red fenders, between the sugary smell of perishky and the smarting wisps of cigarette smoke, between now and last Friday and tomorrow. Between myself and myself.

"For goodness sakes. The boy only gave her a ride home. Why fill her head with all kinds of notions?" This my mother had sung out only to make things infinitely worse. I'd hated the worry in her words.

I'm caught between my mother's common sense and a strange, new, trembling sense of being born from the touch of a boy's hand wrapped around my own and linking me with something wonderful, something my parents wouldn't see. Something they want to keep from me.

I watch my mother rinsing the last soap suds down the kitchen drain. Aunt Frieda says she wishes it would snow so it would seem more like Christmas. My mother nods briskly. "Yes, snow would be nice," she says, "but driving south tomorrow will be easier if the weather stays mild. Anyway, it is Christmas whether it snows or not."

Have to come to Oma's, I sneer to myself. Have to play with cousins. Have to go to Florida tomorrow. What if Larry tries to call? Ten days is so darn long.

I thump the bowl I'm carrying onto the stained table-cloth where the good dishes are being piled until Aunt Frieda takes them to the china cabinet in the middle room.

Who's Janet been with today? What did she mean when she'd whispered during "Hark the Herald Angels" at last night's carol sing—"I've gotta warn you about Larry. Talk to you tomorrow." I pick up a plate and keep rubbing it long after it's dry.

The kitchen smells like burnt candles and sugar icing, reminding me of the school basement at the party on the weekend. I want to hurl myself away from here, away and back to last Friday, to that carol-throbbing moment when the handsomest boy in the whole school had asked me, Linda, to be HIS partner for the party lunch. He'd held my hand as we'd run with the others along the wet, gritty sidewalk from the gym to the candle-lit, locker-lined school basement. He'd eaten two cheese sandwiches and one salami, and said he hated pickles. He told me that "White Christmas" was his favourite Christmas song. Afterwards he'd held my coat for me and then taken me home in his fabulous red convertible.

A red car flashes past the kitchen window into the yard. I bound to the door.

"Hi there. Any grub left?" It's Janet. Some friends have dropped her off. The car, I can see now, is not a convertible.

"Sure, lots." I watch the car back away. The headlights glare at me, and I can't see who's in it.

"Well, close the door, silly. It's freezing out there." Janet rolls her eyes. She turns from me to the aunts at the sink. "Hi everybody! Gee, I'm starved."

Janet is hailed by the aunts as though she's a returning queen. And what's she done to deserve that, I wonder. But I'm glad she's finally come. She's a sort of connection, a witness to last Friday. At least she knows that I am no longer a child.

"So how'd you like the party Friday?" Janet plops jam into the hollow cradle of a zwieback bottom. The women have finished in the kitchen and are talking in the middle room. Every once in a while their laughter bursts against the closed kitchen door, but it's muffled like the sound of the distant TV. The dripping tap and Janet's chewing noises are the only sounds in the room.

"I thought it was a super party." I cup my chin in my hand as I lean on my elbow. This pushes my face directly towards her.

"Well, I didn't. I thought it was crummy. The grade twelves this year have no imagination at all. If you ask me it was a big flop. But then what can you expect at a Mennonite* high school?" Janet peels the skin from a slice of salami. It comes off in an unbroken circle. "I know why you liked it so much. You didn't even notice anything. All you were looking at was that dreamy Larry Enns."

I can feel myself blush, but right now I don't care. I strain to puzzle out the expression on my cousin's face. Is she jealous? Is she happy for me? The muscles around Janet's pencil-thin mouth purse into a slight pucker. It's too blank, too fake. Did she see Larry today? Maybe he talked about me. Janet, say something.

But Janet doesn't.

The cold from the kitchen window lays a penetrating hand on my back. I struggle for something to say. "So what'd you do this afternoon?"

Janet picks up a lemon tart. "Just hung around."

"See anybody special?"

Silence. Then a sigh. "Look, Linda, I hate to tell you this because I don't want to spoil your trip to Florida."

"Tell me what?"

"Well, about Larry."

"What about him?"

"Well, you know he has a girlfriend that goes to Pelee High. You knew that didn't you?"

"Yeah, I know he used to go with somebody. So? He's not married to her."

"Just forget it."

"Good grief. Janet! Forget what? Come on. Tell me what's up."

Another sigh. "Okay. Don't say I didn't warn you. I heard that Larry and his girlfriend had a fight last week, and she was real upset, and so the night of the school party she was out in the parking lot waiting to talk to him. Get it?"

"So? She can sit around and wait." I toss my head back. My hair flicks against the window ledge behind me. I stare hard at the closed kitchen door.

"Gee, you really are immature. Look, Larry knew she was out there. He used you to make her jealous. Now you know." Janet clicks her tongue and scrapes lemon filling from her plate.

"So!" I whirl to face her. "How do you know that's what he was doing? How do you know he cared if she was out there or not?"

Janet clangs the fork down on her plate. "I know, dear cousin, because it obviously worked. I saw them together today, and, believe me, they weren't fighting anymore."

I turn slowly to stare down at the floor. Across the kitchen, the tap drips into the sink—plonk, plonk. It hadn't bothered me before. Plonk, plonk. I squeeze my eyes shut. Plonk, plonk.

I lunge to the sink and wrench both handles of the tap. My hands, gripping the steel knobs, are taut and white. The glow of feeling grown-up has disappeared. I just feel tired.

Voices in the middle room rise up behind the closed door as though someone's turned the volume up.

"Merry Christmas...need a good night's sleep...bright and early."

The kitchen door bursts open, spilling my sister and my mother and father into the room. They've got their coats on. My mother smiles at me and holds up my jacket.

I'm not ready for this intrusion. But there they are—my stiffly smiling mother, my father, and my maddeningly self-satisfied sister Karen, who bounds across the kitchen and flings the door open. "Hey everybody, look. It's snowing!" Crisp air sweeps into the room. Big, fluffy flakes flutter in and settle on the front of her dress.

"Well, look at that, we're getting a white Christmas after all."

"It's beautiful."

Oma and some of the aunts crowd around the door with me and my family. I feel a hand squeeze my elbow. I turn and find Janet close to me. My cousin is staring down at her tightly curled, stockinged toes. "Hey, when you're lying on those gorgeous beaches, don't forget to write a little postcard to your cousin stuck up here in snow country." Janet looks up and wrinkles her nose. She pulls me closer and whispers, "Forget Larry. He's a jerk. You can do better than him."

I blink. The muscles in my throat fight down a tight ache. I search Janet's face for a moment and then we reach for each other and hug. Suddenly I want to hug them all, to bury my face in their coats and show them all it doesn't matter about Larry. But, yes, it does matter very much. And, then again, it doesn't either. I don't know which way I feel. I'm sad-happy to go to Florida. I love-hate Christmas day.

I keep close to my family as we walk across the field towards our house on the next sideroad. The sky is full of big, cottony fluffs that sting my face with cold kisses. I watch them cling to the sleeve of my jacket and melt. Early tomorrow I and my family will whisk past freshly-blanketed fields toward the emerald parks and white, sandy beaches of Florida. I've been there before. Once, when I was just a kid.

"Look at the snow. It'll sure seem different down there now." Karen's voice is happy as she speaks to me.

"Yeah, Florida will be different."

My arm brushes my mother's coat sleeve as we walk. Our shoulders touch. She reaches out and puts her arm around me.

"I know you don't really want to go, Linda. Soon you'll be taking trips of your own." Her sigh is soft. It gets lost in the murmur of the wind whispering secrets to the trees.

My mother's arm squeezes more tightly around me as though for a moment she is trying to push me down and make me small again. Then she lets go. Through my tears the sticky, feathery snowflakes explode into shimmering, long-spindled stars.

* **Oma:** grandmother
* **zwieback:** biscuit or sweetcake, usually toasted
* **perishky:** jam-filled cookie
* **Christmas fesper:** a light, cold supper served on Christmas day; includes sweets
* **crimpolene:** dressmaking material popular in the 1960s and 1970s
* **Opa:** grandfather
* **Trudeau:** prime minister of Canada, 1968-1984
* **Aeltester:** head minister or perhaps elder in a Mennonite congregation
* **Mennonite:** a Protestant religious-cultural group favouring plain dress and plain living, with communities in more than forty countries

Babysittin'

TED RUSSELL

Of all the jobs I've ever done in this world, the one I never want to do agen is babysittin'. Yes, I had a good dory-mate, Grampa Walcott, and we come through safe and sound, but when I think of it—never agen!

Grampa was stuck that night, good and proper. Grandma and her daughter Aunt Sophy, and *her* daughter Soos, who was visitin' from Corner Brook* with her six-months'-old baby, had all been invited out to this special party the Women's Association was givin'—on account of three generations of members bein' here all at the one time.

Of course, they could've got Liz Noddy, Jethro's daughter, to babysit, but Liz would have chewed bubble gum all night, and brought along her grammyphone records (the ones Grampa can't stand). He said a night like that would've drove him cracked. So, that evenin', he asked me if I'd take a berth with him babysittin', and I signed on. Well, from now in, whatever babysittin' there is in Pigeon Inlet*, can be done by Liz Noddy, with her bubble gum, All Shook Up*, Jailhouse Rock* and all the rest of it.

The women had gone when I got there. The baby was sound asleep upstairs and Grampa had the cribbage board all set up on the kitchen table. I asked him did he have any instructions what to do if the baby woke. He said no, Soos had made some funny remark about a formula bein' somewhere, but bein' as how the only formula he knew about was the one for findin' the number of cords in a pile of pulp wood, we figured *that* had no connection with the baby. So we started our game of cribbage.

The women had said they'd be home before ten, but bein' women, there was no sign of 'em at half-past, when the baby started to bawl. We waited to see if the squall'd die down, but it got so bad 'twas likely to frighten all the neighbours, so Grampa went up and brought him down.

When that baby grows up, it won't cost him much in soap to wash his face. All he'd have to do is open his mouth and there'll be no face left to wash. Grampa had him wrong end up when he brought him down, but even after he upended him right, he bawled harder than ever. I made signs to Grampa (there was no sense tryin' to talk), that there must be a pin stickin' in him somewhere. Grampa held him up sort of by the crosstrees*, while I examined among his riggin'*. Next thing I knew, the whole outfit tumbled to the kitchen floor, and there he was in his bare poles,* bawlin', if 'twas possible, harder than ever.

Grampa screeched out something to me about gettin' the canvas* back on him quick, but like I told him, anybody with one eye or for that matter, nar eye at all, could tell we weren't supposed to put *that* back on him. We agreed that the only thing to do was poke it into the kitchen stove and look in the sail locker* for a new outfit. We located the sail locker on top of the sewin' machine and after an argument as to whether we should put a jib* on him or a foresail*, we put *both* of 'em on. Like Grampa said, 'twas best to play safe. The trouble was it only made him bawl more than ever. "There's only one salvation," said Grampa. "Grub. 'Twould have been better," said he, "if Soos had told us what to feed him instead of talkin' about cords of pulpwood."

But what could we feed a young fellow that age? There was cold moose meat in the pantry, but like Grampa said, the rough edges might choke him. Something smooth we wanted, but what? There was only one thing—made to order, you might say. Fat pork. So I took him, while Grampa headed for the pork barrel in the backroom and come back with a lovely little chunk, 'bout half inch each way.

But I had misgivin's. There was no question as to smoothness, or even nourishment. But with no teeth to chew it, supposin' it gave him indigestion. Grampa had the answer to that. Tie a string to it. Then after he'd gone to sleep on it, if it hurt him, we had the wherewithal to get it back.

And that's what we did. He swallered that hunk of salt pork like a real north-shoreman, and before Grampa had him halfway up the stairs he was half asleep, and quiet as a mouse.

'Twas then this horrible thought struck me. Supposin' he swallowed the string too. But when Grampa got downstairs he said as how he'd thought of that very danger, and had belayed the other end of the string to the baby's toe. "But," said I, "when you laid him down didn't he stick up his legs and slacken the string?" "Yes," said Grampa, "he did, and *then* I tied a sheepshank* on it to tighten it again. Then when he dozes off and straightens his legs, up 'twill come, easy as anything."

Five minutes later by Grampa's clock, he creeped up again, and there was the youngster, sound asleep, with his legs straightened out. Grampa untied the string from his toe, picked up the other end off the pillow, and we had both that string and the fat pork in the kitchen stove on top of *that other thing*, just as we heard the women comin' back from the party.

First thing Soos did after we remarked on how quiet the baby was, was to go to the warmin' oven and take out what she called the "formula." And when I saw what it was, I got out of there quick, because the next thing she might do would be to overhaul the contents of the sail locker.

Perhaps, like I told Grampa next day, we shouldn't have burnt *that thing*, but Grampa said "Nonsense! Soo's got so many of 'em she'd never miss one." Besides, what else in the world could we have done with it?

---

* **Corner Brook:** city in the west of Newfoundland
* **Pigeon Inlet:** an imaginary community in Newfoundland
* **"All Shook Up" and "Jailhouse Rock":** two of Elvis Presley's 1957 hits

* **crosstrees, rigging, poles, canvas, sail locker, jib, foresail:** sailing terms; narrator is using an extended metaphor here, comparing the baby to a boat and the diaper to a sail. Hence "crosstrees" are baby's arms, etc.
* **sheepshank:** knot used to shorten rope's length temporarily

Big Brother

SHEKHAR JOSHI

Jagdish Babu saw him for the first time at the small café with the large signboard, on the left coming out of the marketplace. A fair complexion, sparkling eyes, golden-brown hair, and an unusual smooth liveliness in his movements—like a drop of water sliding along the leaf of a lotus. From the alertness in his eyes, one would guess his age at only nine or ten, and that's what it was.

When Jagdish Babu, puffing on a half-lit cigarette, entered the café, the boy was removing some plates from a table. But by the time Jagdish Babu had seated himself at a corner table, the boy was already standing in front of him, looking as though he'd been waiting for hours for him—for a person to sit in that seat. The boy said nothing. He did bow slightly, to show respect, and then just smiled. Receiving the order for a cup of tea, he smiled again, went off, and then returned with the tea in the twinkling of an eye.

Feelings are strange. Even isolated in a solitary and deserted place, a man may feel no loneliness. Despite the isolation, everything is very intimate, very much his own. In contrast, though, there is sometimes a feeling of loneliness even in a bustling setting among thousands of people. Everything there seems alien, lacking in intimacy. But that feeling of solitude and isolation inevitably has roots in a history of separation or detachment.

Jagdish Babu had come from a distant region and was alone. In the hustle and bustle of the marketplace, in the clamor of the café, everything seemed unrelated to himself. Maybe after living here for a while and growing accustomed to it, he'd start feeling some intimacy in the surroundings. But today the place seemed alien, beyond the boundary of belonging—far beyond. Then he began remembering nostalgically the people of his village region, the school and college boys there, the café in the nearby town.

"Tea, Sha'b!"

Jagdish Babu flicked the ash from his cigarette. In the boy's pronunciation of "Sahab*," he sensed something which he had been missing. He proceeded to follow up the speculation— "What's your name?"

"Madan."

"Very well, Madan! Where are you from?"

"I'm from the hills, Babuji*."

"There are hundreds of hill places—Abu, Darjeeling, Mussoorie, Simla, Almora. Which hills is your village in?"

"Almora, Sha'b," he said with a smile, "Almora."

"Which village in Almora?" he persisted.

The boy hesitated. Perhaps embarrassed by the strange name of the village, he answered evasively—"Oh it's far away, Sha'b. It must be fifteen or twenty miles from Almora."

"But it still must have a name," Jagdish Babu insisted.

"Dotyalgaon," he responded shyly.

The strain of loneliness vanished from Jagdish Babu's face, and when he smiled and told Madan that he was from a neighboring village, the boy almost dropped his tray with delight. He stood there speechless and dazed, as though trying to recall his past.

The past: a village...high mountains...a stream...mother ...father...older sister...younger sister...big brother.

Whose shadow was it that Madan saw reflected in the form of Jagdish Babu? Mother?—No. Father?—No. Elder or younger sister?—No. Big brother?—Yes, Dajyu!

Within a few days, the gap of unfamiliarity between Madan and Jagdish Babu had disappeared. As soon as the gentleman sat down, Madan would call out—"Greetings, Dajyu!"

"Dajyu, it's very cold today." "Dajyu, will it snow here too?" "Dajyu, you didn't eat much yesterday."

Then from some direction would come a cry—"Boy!" And Madan would be there even before the echo of the call could be heard. Leaving with the order, he would ask Jagdish Babu, "Anything for you, Dajyu?"

"Bring me some water."

"Right away, Dajyu," Madan would call out from the other end of the room, repeating the word "Dajyu" with the eagerness and affection of a mother embracing her son after a long separation.

After some time, Jagdish Babu's loneliness disappeared. Now not only the marketplace and the café but the city itself seemed painted with a sense of belonging. Madan's constant cry of "Dajyu" ringing out from all over the room, however, no longer pleased him.

"Madan! Come here."

"Coming, Dajyu!"

This repetition of the word "Dajyu" aroused the bourgeois temperament in Jagdish Babu. The thin thread of intimacy could not survive the strong pull of ego.

"Shall I bring tea, Dajyu?"

"No tea. But what's this 'Dajyu, Dajyu' you keep shouting all the time? Have you no respect for a person's prestige?"

Jagdish Babu, flushed with anger, had no control over his words. Nor did he stop to wonder whether Madan could know the meaning of "prestige." But Madan, even with no explanation, had understood everything. Could one who had braved an understanding of the world at such a tender age fail to comprehend one paltry word?

Having made the excuse of a headache to the manager, Madan sat in his small room, head between his knees, and sobbed. In these circumstances far from home, his display of intimacy toward Jagdish Babu had been perfectly natural. But now, for the first time in a foreign place, he felt as though someone had pulled him from the lap of his mother, from the arms of his father, and from the protection of his sister.

Madan returned to his work as before.

The next day, heading for the café, Jagdish Babu suddenly met a childhood friend, Hemant. Reaching the café, Jagdish Babu beckoned to Madan, but he sensed that the boy was trying to remain at a distance. On the second call, Madan finally came over.

Today that smile was not on his face, nor did he say, "What can I bring, Dajyu?" Jagdish Babu himself had to speak up—"Two teas, two omelets."

Even then, instead of replying, "Right away, Dajyu," he said, "Right away, Sha'b," and then left, as though the man were a stranger.

"Perhaps a hill boy?" Hemant speculated.

"Yes," muttered Jagdish Babu and changed the subject.

Madan had brought the tea.

"What's your name?" Hemant asked, as though trying to be friendly.

For a few moments silence engulfed the table. Jagdish Babu's lowered eyes were centered on the cup of tea. Memories swam before Madan's eyes—Jagdish Babu asking his name like this one day...then, "Dajyu, you didn't eat much yesterday"...and one day, "You pay no attention to anyone's prestige...."

Jagdish Babu raised his eyes and saw that Madan seemed about to erupt like a volcano.

"What's your name?" Hemant repeated insistently.

"Sha'b, they call me 'Boy,'" he said quickly and walked away.

"A real blockhead," Hemant remarked, taking a sip of tea. "He can't even remember his own name."

* **Sahab:** sir, mister
* **Babuji:** the "ji" added to Babu's
  name indicates respect

Tayzanne

Retold by DIANE WOLKSTEIN

Every day, either Velina or her younger brother went to the spring to bring back water. One morning, when Velina dipped her bucket into the water, her ring fell off. Ahh-hh. The waters stirred. Up came a great silver-golden fish.

"Have you seen my ring?" Velina asked.

The fish disappeared into the waters and came up again with Velina's ring on his nose.

"Oh, thank you," said the girl. "My name is Velina. I live nearby and come almost every day to the spring for water. But I did not know you lived here."

The fish said, "My name is Tayzanne. I live in the deepest part of the spring. If you would like, I will take your bucket and bring you water that is cool and sweet."

Velina held out her bucket and the fish took it and disappeared under the spring. Down he went. Down and down. And then he appeared again with Velina's bucket filled with clear, sweet water. Velina thanked him and went home.

After some days, the girl's mother noticed that the water Velina brought back from the spring was always clearer than that which her brother brought back. She spoke to the little boy and told him to pay more attention to where he got his water. Several days later, she saw it was still muddy. She scolded the boy and said,

"I told you to pay more attention when you dip your bucket into the water. I want you to bring back water as clear as your sister's."

So the little boy decided to follow Velina the next morning to see where she dipped her bucket into the water. He walked quietly behind Velina, and hid behind a tree, and watched as Velina came to the edge of the spring and sang:

> Tayzanne, fish of the clear spring,
> Tayzanne, fish of the deep.
> Tayzanne, my friend.
> My friend, Tayzanne, Tayzanne,
> Tayzanne, my friend,
> O come to me.

Then he went home and told his mother that the next day he could bring back water as clear as Velina's.

"How will you do it?" his mother asked.

"It will be easy. I will do as Velina. I will sing to the fish in the spring and when he comes out I will give him my bucket and he will give me clear, sweet water just as he does for Velina."

"No, no," said the mother. "You must not do that. That is an evil spirit who lives in the water. I will go myself."

That evening the mother followed Velina to the spring. She hid and listened as Velina sang:

> Tayzanne, fish of the clear spring,
> Tayzanne, fish of the deep.
> Tayzanne, my friend,
> My friend, Tayzanne, Tayzanne,
> Tayzanne, my friend,
> O come to me.

Then she saw the silver-golden fish leap from the waters and take Velina's bucket and return with it filled with water. She went home.

But Tayzanne, through his powers, understood the mother's intentions, and told Velina that her mother would try to kill him. He told her that if she saw three drops of blood on her breast she would know that her mother had succeeded. Velina started to cry when she heard this, but Tayzanne said she need not worry for in the end they would be together.

The mother told her husband that there was an evil spirit in the spring who was consorting with their daughter and that they must kill it the next day.

In the morning, Velina's mother sent her to market to sell vegetables. Velina did not want to go, but she had to obey. The mother and father and the little boy went to the spring. In a stern voice the mother sang:

> Tayzanne, fish of the clear spring,
> Tayzanne, fish of the deep.
> Tayzanne, my friend,
> My friend, Tayzanne, Tayzanne,
> Tayzanne, my friend,
> O come to me.

There was no movement in the waters. "You sing," she said to her son, "your voice is lighter. It is closer to Velina's." The boy sang softly:

> Tayzanne, fish of the clear spring,
> Tayzanne, fish of the deep.
> Tayzanne, my friend,
> My friend, Tayzanne, Tayzanne,
> Tayzanne, my friend,
> O come to me.

The fish leaped up. He was very large. The father threw the rope he had brought with him. He threw it like a lasso and caught the silver-golden fish. But the fish was so powerful it did not die. The father had to take out his machete to kill it.

Velina was sad all day. In the afternoon her breast felt damp. She thought it was her tears, but when she looked down at her white blouse she saw three drops of blood. Quickly she gathered together her vegetables and went home. She entered the house and saw her mother was cooking a large fish over the fire. She ran out. She ran to the spring. She sang:

> Tayzanne, fish of the clear spring,
> Tayzanne, fish of the deep.
> Tayzanne, my friend,
> My friend, Tayzanne, Tayzanne,
> Tayzanne, my friend,
> O come to me.

The waters were still. Velina went home. But she would not enter the house. She sat on a chair outside. She began to comb her hair. Looking into a small mirror and combing her hair, she sang and she wept:

Tayzanne, fish of the clear spring,
Tayzanne, fish of the deep.
Tayzanne, my friend,
My friend, Tayzanne, Tayzanne,
Tayzanne, my friend,
O come to me.

Her brother heard her singing and came out. Ah. What he saw. The chair she was sitting on was sinking into the earth.

"Velina! Velina, stop crying," he said. "Your tears are softening the earth."

But Velina was so filled with sadness she did not hear him.

The brother ran inside. "Papa, Papa, come quick. Velina is sinking into the earth."

"It is late," the father answered. "You are imagining things, go to bed."

"But Papa, please, please."

The brother ran outside again. Velina had sunk into the earth up to her waist.

"Mama, Mama, Mama," he cried, "you must come, Velina is sinking into the earth."

"Nonsense," said the mother, but the boy pleaded so desperately that she went outside just as Velina's shoulders sank into the earth. The mother ran and grabbed her daughter by the hair, but the rest of her had already been swallowed up. The mother stood there and the brother too, in the night—and all that was left was Velina's hair.

With Friends Like These...

BARRY DANIELS

Ephraim Bedloe and me go way back, you know. Lived all our lives in this valley; went to school together, and farmed next door to each other for nigh on half a century. So it's natural that folks should come to me for the truth of it: "Was it all truly a misunderstanding," they ask me, "or did the old coot plan the whole thing right from the beginning?"

Well it pains me to have to say this—but I don't know. I've lost count of the times I've asked him, was it all just a misunderstanding or did you know what you were doing all along? He looks me straight in the eye and he says, "George, 'twas all no more than a mix up which by the grace of God turned out all right in the end." Then, when I think I've the truth of it at last, he'll give me one of those great broad winks of his that crinkles up the whole side of his face and a great silly grin like a lad caught with his finger in the cherry pie.

Maybe the only way to get at the truth is to reason it out, like Sherlock Holmes would, or that scruffy detective on TV. "Let's just stick with the facts, ma'am," he'll say, and then he'll reason out the whole mystery and you just want to kick yourself for not having seen it all along.

The shot was a fact. Booming out of the still, spring morning and rolling like thunder along the blue hills to the end of the valley and echoing back down the river. Tommy Faulkner was up by then, and he heard it plain as day. Set the crows to squawkin', it did, and brought old Millie Faulkner out of her kitchen at a run.

Old Millie, she's not much on brains, and I reckon she was at the back of the line when they handed out good looks too, but she got her big mouth right at the front of the line, and a nose she's always sticking into other people's business. Still, the good Lord gave Millie a heart to match the size of her mouth and on account of the one, folks tend to overlook the other, if you catch my drift. She means well, Millie does. I guess that could be the epitaph of many a busybody.

Anyways, when Millie hears the shot she waits only long enough for Tom to point her in the right direction and she's a-throwin' off her apron and jumpin' into that old Chevy pickup of theirs to go see what's up.

Now the last thing that Ephraim needed that morning was a visit from Millie Faulkner, and you can put that down for another fact, but Millie came a-rattlin' down the drive, kickin' up the dust with that old pickup, and pulled in by the porch just as Eph came up over the fields. He was carrying his shotgun in one hand, a long-handled spade in the other, and his hands were covered in blood to the wrists. It takes a lot to stop up Millie's yappin', but Eph managed it that morning; for a while.

Millie was half scared out of her wits, and I'll tell you that don't leave a lot of wits left. Well, like it does with many folk, scared came out angry and she laid into Ephraim, demanding to know where Mary was—Eph's missus, that is. Eph mumbled something about Mary takin' off to visit her sister, and told Millie to mind her own damned business anyway. Now telling Millie to mind her own business is a red rag to a bull and she really started on into Eph at that point, which is just about exactly the last thing you should do to a man carrying a shotgun and covered in blood. Eph put down the spade, but hung onto the gun, and turned to Millie all calm and quiet (which scared her more than if he'd been a-rantin' and a-ravin' at her) and he said, almost in a whisper: "Now go easy on me, Millie, or dammit I'll be diggin' two graves out there this day instead of just the one."

And then she looked him square in the eye and noticed the tears, streamin' down both his cheeks, and that scared old Millie more than anything else on that strange morning. She jumped right back in her old pickup and left Eph in a cloud of dust and exhaust smoke, with the tears still coming.

Eph's no fool, of course, so he knew what had to come next. He put away his shotgun, fetched a beer from the icebox, sat himself out on the porch looking over his front fifteen acres, and settled in to wait for a visit from Jake Mundt. Sheriff Mundt, that is; our local version of that TV cop. Eph knew that was where Millie was roaring off to, and he was dead right.

Now here's another of those Sherlock Holmes-type "facts of the case": It concerns that fifteen-acre parcel out front of Eph's farmhouse, the one he was a-gazin' at while he waited for Mundt.

Fact is, I've seen a lot of land go under the plough in my day, and I'm telling you that parcel of land has got to be the hardest, stoniest, meanest piece of God's earth that ever broke a steel blade. Eph had been trying for years to put it under the plough, but all he'd got to show for it was another busted transmission on his tractor. That needed major surgery this time—costly surgery by the look of it—so the tractor was up on blocks, waiting for Eph to somehow find the funds to bring in a professional mechanic.

Eph sat, sipped, stared and waited. Mundt arrived about forty minutes later. He got down from his car, fetched himself a cold beer and sat down on the porch step. Eph gave the sheriff "Good Mornin'" and the two sat awhile, watchin' the sun glint off the rocks, and old Jake never mentioned the gun nor the blood on Eph's hands. Two old friends sharing some time together. Then Mundt says:

"Where is she, Eph?"

"Millie Faulkner's an old fool," says Ephraim.

"No denying that," says Jake Mundt. "Now where's your Mary? And don't start that tale about visiting her sister, 'cause I called already and there ain't no visit nor no plans to visit. Want to take it from there, Ephraim?"

Eph said nothing, sipped, rocked back and forth, stared out over his land. Mundt got up and squinted out under the sun.

"There's fresh-turned earth out there, Eph. Thinking on putting in some tomatoes, were you?"

Not a word from Eph. He stood, shrugged, turned slowly, and went into the house. Mundt opened the leather restraining strap on his gun, and moved to the porch. Eph came out of the house holding his shotgun, but it was open and he held it by the barrel. He gave Jake the gun and held out his wrists for the cuffs.

"Want to tell me where to dig?" Mundt asked.

Eph moved to the car. He didn't say nothin' then, and he added precious little later.

Jake put Eph in a cell on Monday morning, and there he stayed 'til Thursday noon when he was bundled into the police car and driven back to his property to meet with this policeman, this Morrison, a detective he was, out from the city. Not at all like the fellow on the TV. A little fellow, Morrison was, all points and sharp edges. Talked fast and moved in quick dashes, like he was always anxious to be somewhere other than where he was. I had a dog like that once.

Morrison starts in on Eph, asking whereabouts Mary might be, but nasty like, not with any concern at all. We all thought that the suspect was supposed to be innocent until proved guilty, but this Morrison had it backwards. "Where'd you bury the body?" he kept asking.

Eph wasn't paying much attention to the detective, anyway. He was much more interested in the twenty or thirty men they'd set to digging holes all about his rocky acres. They had these big, orange-colored earthmovers in, and men with picks breaking up rocks and hauling them away in wheelbarrows.

Jake had no love for this Morrison, I can tell you. He'd gotten himself bawled out by Morrison in front of his deputies, 'cause somebody let Eph wash himself up in the cell afore anybody thought to take samples of the blood from his fingers. Anyway, as Jake tells it, Morrison was talking to Eph at a rate of thirteen to the dozen, but Eph was just a-starin' over the field with a strange look in his eye.

"Where'd you bury her, Bedloe?" Morrison asked for about the fifth time. "It'll go better with you if you help us. Where'd you bury your wife? We've got Millie Faulkner's testimony, we've two neighbors heard the shotgun, and we've marked the spots where the ground's been turned. We'll dig them all if we have to, but why don't you make it easy on us, and on yourself as well. Where's the body, Bedloe?"

Eph stared at the men in the field for long seconds before replying and when he did, it was real slow-like, as though choosing each word very carefully. "Well inspector, I'll tell you this," Eph said, "I may look like a dumb sod-farmer but I'm not so stupid as I'd plant a flag where I'd buried a body. Speaking—

how do you say it?—'hype-a-thetical,' if I'd done what you're saying I done, I reckon I'd have dug those little holes all over just to throw some jackass like you off the scent. Hype-a-thetical, of course."

And that was it. Not another word could they get out of Eph, and in the end the little inspector got tired first and sent Jake to take Eph back to his cell. Some say Jake was a-grinnin' all the way home.

Come Saturday morning, sunlight through the small, barred window woke Eph early and he got up to stretch some feeling back into his arms and legs, which had gotten cramped from the small cot. He washed his face with cold water and shaved as best he could, trying to keep the nicks and scratches to a minimum. At nine a.m., he rattled his bars and called for Mundt.

"What you want, Eph?"

"Got to get out of here, Jake."

"You going to confess? Is that what you mean? You want me to call Morrison?"

"That little jackass?" Eph laughed. "The hell with him; I got to get me down to the bus station by ten o'clock. Now open this cage before I got to pull the damn door off."

"Why you got to get to the bus station, Eph? You planning on taking a trip, or something?"

"Come on, Jake, open up. I got to get down there to meet the ten o'clock bus in from the city. Mary's on that bus, and she'll have a blue fit if I'm not there to meet her. Move, now Jake. You know my Mary's temper. Do *you* want to be the one to explain why I couldn't get down to the bus to meet her?"

Eph says it's a toss-up who was the more surprised: Mary, to see old Mundt waitin' to meet her, or Mundt to see Mary skippin' down from the bus, glowin' with good health and jumpin' up to give Eph a big kiss, like a young girl on her honeymoon.

Jake no doubt thought he'd get the mystery out of Eph later, but he never did. Eph didn't like the way he'd been treated by some of his so-called "friends" and he decided to let them stew for a while. But he told me and, if you promise not to spread it around too far, I'll tell you.

First off there's a part of the secret that'll be out in a few months anyway, when Mary's middle starts to show. Now Mary is one fine, healthy woman, and bearin' another child shouldn't by rights be a problem; but she is getting on in years—no, I'm damned if I'll tell you how many—so she'd been away to the city hospital for a week of tests and observation. Well, she brought back two pieces of information: The baby is healthy—and it's a boy. The news just took ten years off Ephraim Bedloe, let me tell you.

Nat'rally Mary didn't want the news up and down the valley afore she was ready—you know how women are about these things—so the very last person Eph would have told was Millie Faulkner, even if she'd come at a good time.

Which she didn't. Millie showed up at the worst possible time.

Eph's old dog, Jenny, had been ailin' bad for some months back, you see. She was nearly fifteen, Jenny was, and that's a fine span for a dog. Well, the vet had told Eph what had to be done, but he'd put it off as long as he could—which was right up to that Monday morning, after a long and sleepless night. She never felt a thing, Jenny didn't. One shot.

The best part of the story, of course, is how Ephraim had finally got his rocky fifteen ploughed. Eph says that when his old truck turned off the highway and Mary saw the east fifteen, she squealed and jumped about so, he was worried for their unborn son. Give them their due, the police had put the land back to rights. The last of the big equipment had moved out just a few minutes earlier.

"Oh, Eph; how'd you do it?" Mary asked. "Did you fix the tractor...?"

"No, honey" Eph told her. "I got a little help from some friends!"

So now you've all of the facts. There's a fine crop of corn starting to show out of the rocky fifteen, and with luck the land will finally start to repay Eph for the hard work he's put into it over the years. Did he plan the whole thing? Or did fate and cir-cumstance throw it into his lap?

I'm damned if I know; and I'll probably never find out. I bet that TV cop would have reasoned the whole thing out by now.

Sucker

CARSON MCCULLERS

It was always like I had a room to myself. Sucker slept in my bed with me but that didn't interfere with anything. The room was mine and I used it as I wanted to. Once I remember sawing a trap door in the floor. Last year when I was a sophomore in high school I tacked some pictures of girls on the walls. My mother never bothered me because she had the younger kids to look after. And Sucker thought anything I did was always swell.

Whenever I'd bring any of my friends back to my room all I had to do was just glance once at Sucker and he'd get up from whatever he was busy with and maybe half smile at me, and leave without saying a word. He never brought kids back here. He's twelve, four years younger than I am, and he always knew without me even telling him that I didn't want kids that age meddling with my things.

Half the time I used to forget that Sucker isn't my brother. He's my first cousin, but practically ever since I can remember he's been in our family. You see, his folks were killed in a wreck when he was a baby. To me and my kid sisters he was like our brother.

Sucker used to remember and believe every word I said. That's how he got his nickname. Once a couple of years ago I told him that if he'd jump off our garage with an umbrella it would act as a parachute and he wouldn't fall hard. He did it and busted his knee. That's just one instance. And the funny thing was that no matter how many times he got fooled he would still believe me. Not that he was dumb in other ways—it was just the way he acted with me.

There is one thing I have learned, but it makes me feel guilty and is hard to figure out. If a person admires you a lot, you despise him and don't care—and it is the person who doesn't notice you that you are apt to admire. This is not easy to realize.

Maybelle Watts, this senior at school, acted like she was the Queen of Sheba. Yet at the same time I would have done anything in the world to get her attention. When Sucker was a little kid and on up until the time he was twelve, I guess I treated him as bad as Maybelle did me.

Now that Sucker has changed so much it is a little hard to remember him as he used to be. I never imagined I'd want to think back and compare and try to get things straight in my mind. If I could have seen ahead, maybe I would have acted different.

I never noticed him much, and when you consider how long we have had the same room together it is funny the few things I remember. He used to talk to himself a lot when he'd think he was alone—all about him fighting gangsters and being on ranches and that sort of kid stuff. Usually, though, he was very quiet. He didn't have many boys in the neighborhood to buddy with, and his face had the look of a kid who is watching a game and waiting to be asked to play. That is how I remember him—getting a little bigger every year, but still being the same. That was Sucker up until a few months ago, when all this trouble began.

Maybelle was somehow mixed up in what happened, so I guess I ought to start with her. Until I knew her I hadn't given much time to girls. Last fall she sat next to me in General Science class and that was when I first began to notice her. Her hair is the brightest yellow I ever saw and sometimes she wears it set into curls with some sort of gluey stuff. Her fingernails are pointed and painted a shiny red. All during class I used to watch Maybelle, except when I thought she was going to look my way or when the teacher called on me. Her hands are very little and white except for that red stuff, and when she would turn the pages of her book she always licked her thumb and held out her little finger and turned very slowly.

It is impossible to describe Maybelle. All the boys are crazy about her, but she didn't even notice me. For one thing she's almost two years older than I am. Between periods I used to try and pass very close to her in the halls, but she would hardly ever smile at me.

Even at night I would think about Maybelle. Sometimes Sucker would wake up and ask me why I couldn't get settled and I'd tell him to hush his mouth. I guess I wanted to ignore somebody like Maybelle did me. You could always tell by Sucker's face when his feelings were hurt. I don't remember all the ugly remarks I must have made, because even when I was saying them my mind was on Maybelle.

That went on for nearly three months and then somehow she began to change. In the halls she would speak to me and every morning she copied my homework. Then one lunchtime I danced with her in the gym, and knew everything was going to change.

It was that night when this trouble really started. I had come into my room late and Sucker was already asleep. I felt happy and keyed up and was awake thinking about Maybelle a long time. Then I dreamed about her and it seemed I kissed her. It was a surprise to wake up and see the dark. The house was quiet, and Sucker's voice was a shock.

"Pete?..." I didn't answer anything or even move.

"You do like me as if I was your own brother, don't you, Pete?"

I couldn't get over the surprise, and it was like this was the real dream instead of the other.

"You have liked me all the time like I was your own brother, haven't you?"

"Sure," I said.

Sucker felt little and warm against my back, and his warm breath touched my shoulder.

"No matter what you did I always knew you liked me."

I was wide awake and my mind seemed mixed up in a strange way. I guess you understand people better when you are happy than when something is worrying you. It was like I had never really thought about Sucker until then. I felt I had always been mean to him. One night a few weeks before I had heard him crying in the dark. He said he had lost a boy's beebee gun and was scared to let anybody know. He wanted me to tell him what to do. I was sleepy and tried to make him hush and when he wouldn't I kicked at him. That was just one of the things I remembered.

"You're a swell kid, Sucker," I said.

It seemed to me suddenly that I did like him more than anybody else I knew—more than any other boy, more than my sisters, more in a certain way even than Maybelle. I felt good all over and it was like when they play sad music in the movies. I wanted to show Sucker how much I really thought of him and make up for the way I had always treated him.

We talked for a good while that night. His voice was fast and it was like he had been saving up these things to tell me for a long time. He mentioned that he was going to try to build a canoe and that the kids down the block wouldn't let him in on their football team and I don't know what all. I talked some too, and it was a good feeling to think of him taking in everything I said so seriously. I even spoke of Maybelle a little, only I made out like it was her who had been running after me all this time. He asked questions about high school and so forth. His voice was excited and he kept on talking fast like he could never get the words out in time. When I went to sleep he was still talking.

During the next couple of weeks I saw a lot of Maybelle. She acted as though she really cared for me a little. Half the time I felt so good I hardly knew what to do with myself.

But I didn't forget about Sucker. There were a lot of old things in my bureau drawer I'd been saving—boxing gloves and second-rate fishing tackle. All this I turned over to him. We had some more talks and it was really like I was knowing him for the first time. When there was a long cut on his cheek I knew he had been monkeying around with this new razor set of mine, but I didn't say anything.

His face seemed different now. He used to look timid and sort of like he was afraid of a whack over the head. That expression was gone. His face, with those wide-open eyes and his ears sticking out and his mouth never quite shut, had the look of a person who is surprised and expecting something swell.

Once I started to point him out to Maybelle and tell her he was my kid brother. It was an afternoon when a murder mystery was on at the movie. I had earned a dollar working for my dad and I gave Sucker a quarter to go and get candy and so forth. With the rest I took Maybelle. We were sitting near the back and I saw Sucker come in. He began to stare at the screen the minute he stepped past the ticket man and he stumbled down the aisle without noticing where he was going. I started to punch Maybelle, but Sucker looked a little silly—walking with his eyes glued to the movie and wiping his reading glasses on his shirttail. He went on until he got to the first few rows where the kids usually sit. It felt good to have both of them at the movie with the money I earned.

I guess things went on like this for about a month or six weeks, with me feeling so good I couldn't settle down to study or put my mind on anything. I wanted to be friendly with everybody. There were times when I just had to talk to some person. And usually that would be Sucker. He felt as good as I did. Once he said: "Pete, I am glad you are like my brother. It makes me gladder than anything else in the world."

Then something happened between Maybelle and me. I never have figured out just what it was. She began to act different. At first I tried to think it was just my imagination, but she didn't act glad to see me anymore. I'd see her out riding with this fellow on the football team who has a yellow car the color of her hair. After school she would ride off with him, laughing and looking into his face.

I couldn't think of anything to do about it and she was on my mind all day and night. When I did get a chance to go out with her she was snippy and didn't seem to notice me. This made me feel like something was the matter—I'd worry about my shoes clopping too loud on the floor or the bumps on my chin.

At first I was so worried I just forgot about Sucker. Then later he began to get on my nerves. He was always hanging around until I would get back from high school, with his waiting expression on his face. Then I wouldn't say anything or I'd maybe answer him rough-like and he would finally go out.

I can't divide that time up and say this happened one day and that the next. For one thing, I was so mixed up the weeks just slid along into each other. Maybelle still rode around with this fellow and sometimes she would smile at me and sometimes not. Every afternoon I went from one place to another where I thought she'd be.

Sucker kept getting on my nerves more and more. He looked as though he sort of blamed me for something, but at the same time knew that it wouldn't last long. He was growing fast and for some reason began to stutter. Sometimes he had nightmares or would lose his breakfast. Mom got him a bottle of cod-liver oil.

Then the finish came between Maybelle and me. I met her going to the drugstore and asked for a date. When she said no, I said something sarcastic. She told me she was sick and tired of my being around and that she had never cared a rap about me. I just stood there and didn't answer anything. I walked home slowly.

For several afternoons I stayed in my room by myself. I didn't want to go anywhere or talk to anyone. When Sucker would come in and look at me sort of funny I'd yell at him to get out. I didn't want to think of Maybelle and I sat at my desk reading or whittling at a toothbrush rack I was making. It seemed to me I was putting that girl out of my mind pretty well.

But you can't help what happens to you at night. That is what made things how they are now.

You see, I dreamed about Maybelle again. It was like the first time and Sucker woke up. He reached for my hand.

"Pete, what's the matter with you?"

All of a sudden I felt so mad my throat choked—at myself and the dream and Maybelle and Sucker and every single person I knew. I remembered all the times Maybelle had humiliated me and everything bad that ever happened. It was as if nobody would ever like me but a sap like Sucker.

"Why is it we aren't buddies like we were before? Why—?"

"Shut your trap!" I jumped up and turned on the light. He sat in the middle of the bed, his eyes blinking and scared.

There was something in me and I couldn't help myself. I don't think anybody ever gets that mad but once. Words came without me knowing what they would be. It was only afterward that I remembered each thing I said.

"Why aren't we buddies? Because you're the dumbest slob I ever saw! Nobody cares anything about you! And just because I felt sorry for you sometimes and tried to act decent, don't think I gave a darn for a dumb little creep like you!"

If I'd talked loud or hit him it wouldn't have been so bad. But my voice was slow and like I was very calm. Sucker's mouth was part-way open and he looked as though he'd knocked his funny bone. His face was white and sweat came out on his forehead. He wiped it away with the back of his hand and for a minute his arm stayed raised that way as if holding something away from him.

"Don't you know a single thing? Haven't you ever been around at all? Why don't you get a girl friend instead of me? What kind of a sissy do you want to grow up to be, anyway?"

I didn't know what was coming next. I couldn't help my-self or think. Sucker didn't move. He had on one of my pajama jackets and his neck stuck out skinny and small. His hair was damp on his forehead.

"Why do you always hang around me? Don't you know when you're not wanted?"

Afterward I could remember the change in Sucker's face. Slowly that blank look went away and he closed his mouth. His eyes got narrow and his fists shut. I'd never seen such a look on him before. It was like every second he was getting older—a hard look to his eyes that seemed wrong in a kid. A drop of sweat rolled down his chin and he didn't notice. He just sat with those eyes on me and didn't speak and his face didn't move.

"No, you don't know when you're not wanted. You're too dumb, just like your name—a dumb Sucker."

It was like something had busted inside me. I turned off the lights and sat down by the window. My legs were shaking and I was so tired I could have bawled. I sat there a long time. After a while I heard Sucker lie down.

I wasn't mad anymore, only tired. It seemed awful to me that I had talked like that to a kid only twelve. I couldn't take it all in. I told myself I would go over to him and try to make it up. But I just sat there in the cold. I planned how I could straighten it out in the morning. Then, trying not to squeak the springs, I got back in bed.

Sucker was gone when I woke up the next day. And later, when I wanted to apologize as I had planned, he looked at me in this new hard way so that I couldn't say a word.

All of that was two or three months ago. Since then Sucker has grown faster than anybody I ever saw. He's almost as tall as I am and his bones have gotten heavier and bigger. He won't wear my old clothes anymore.

Our room isn't mine at all now. He's gotten up this gang of kids and they have a club. When they aren't digging trenches in some vacant lot and fighting, they are always in my room. They've rigged up a radio and every afternoon it blares out music.

It's even worse when we are alone together in the room. He sprawls across the bed and just stares at me with that hard, half-sneering look. I fiddle around my desk and can't get settled. The thing is, I have to study because I've gotten three bad cards this term already. If I flunk English I can't graduate next year. I don't want to be a bum and I just have to get my mind on it.

I don't care a flip for Maybelle anymore, and it's only this thing between Sucker and me that is the trouble now. We never speak except when we have to before the family. I don't even want to call him Sucker anymore, and unless I forget I call him by his real name, Richard. At night I can't study with him in the room and I have to hang around the drugstore with fellows who loaf there.

More than anything I want to be easy in my mind again. And I miss the way Sucker and I were for a while in a funny, sad way that before this I never would have believed. But everything is so different that there seems to be nothing I can do to get it right. I've sometimes thought if we could have it out in a big fight that would help. But I can't fight him because he's four years younger. And another thing—sometimes this look in his eyes makes me almost believe that if Sucker could, he would kill me.

The Visitor

PUNYAKANTE WIJENAIKE

There is only one thing about Mrs. Dias that could be called abnormal and that is her complete lack of emotion. Her corpulent self is stolid almost to the point of boredom. Mrs. Dias is my new boarder. My purse strings need no stretching for my little business is thriving and there is always money in the till. Besides, living is cheap for a lone woman. One does not have to eat at regular meal times because cooking for one's self becomes too much of a bother to indulge in frequently. But I am lonely. The house stands alone at the foot of a hill and though cars go up and down the road, from Colombo* up to Kandy* and from Kandy down to Colombo, still one can be very lonely. So I advertised my spare room and the only one who answered the advertisement was Mrs. Dias. I had no choice but to accept her. When one is lonely one accepts anything at all.

But loneliness can have its advantages too. I believe I am a good cook. The only cook within a radius of ten to fifteen miles of good road. By the simple process of turning out hot hoppers* with egg, or string-hoppers* with mulligatawny*, I have managed to live very well indeed. If twenty cars go by for a day, at least ten would stop at the sight of the painted board outside my gate. I had regular customers too. Men who made it a habit of taking the business down to Colombo always stopped for a hot hopper.

The morning Mrs. Dias came I had just finished serving a customer with his breakfast. She came in a hired car overflowing with her belongings. Half a dozen suitcases piled one on top of the other, cooking-pots, pillows, brown paper parcels and even an old mattress with the cotton peeping out in places. Amid all this confusion Mrs. Dias sat calm and unruffled holding her best parasol. But that was typical of Mrs. Dias. She never worried about anything and didn't expect anyone else to do it either. A room was advertised and she came prepared to take it. Never did she once worry whether the room had been already let out or whether it would suit her taste. She never wrote and informed me that she was coming. She simply came.

I have often wondered what she would have done if I refused to take her in. As far as I could judge she was not rich enough to throw money on a return trip to Colombo. And it was apparent that she had given up her previous lodgings and come with all her possessions packed in the car. I do not know whether she was stupid or merely indifferent to what might have happened to her if she was turned away. At the most she may have been mildly surprised and then gone on to a rest-house to contemplate the next move in her stolid fashion.

She was fully satisfied with the room. She never said so in words, Mrs. Dias never expressed what she felt, but I could see that she had no complaints in the way she moved about, plodding systematically from suitcase to wardrobe, neatly arranging her clothes in separate piles. She had brought quite a number of little knick-knacks wrapped in cotton wool which she now arranged on the little table in the centre of the room. Little bits of brightly coloured glass which a child would treasure. Dogs, cats, fish, a shepherd and shepherdess and a tiny musical box shaped like a piano. Her hands moved over them lovingly as if they were the most expensive of crystal. In the windows she hung dark brown curtains and spread a purple satin cover on the bed. The cover had a huge pink rose painted in the middle. Her clothes were of the plainest and sometimes she would wear a blue saree* with a brown jacket and be perfectly satisfied.

Mrs. Dias and I soon fell into a routine which never changed its course. Sharp at seven-thirty she would come to breakfast, dressed oddly, her still black hair oiled back into a neat *konde.** Though her hair had no grey streaks, her body was soft and flabby with flesh that shook and quivered when she moved. Her plump cheeks were bits of dough into which her mild brown eyes were sunk.

She would bid me good morning then fix her eyes firmly on the food. Between mouthfuls she would interrupt herself to put banal questions such as:

"Are the string-hoppers soft today?" or "Are you making meat or fish curry for the hoppers?" "I do hope it will not rain and spoil things."

The questions never varied. After breakfast she would potter around the kitchen probing and touching everything that came her way. She did not do this through inquisitiveness or interest but simply as a matter of routine. Once she upset the batter I had made down the front of her clean saree.

"Do not worry about it dear," she said in a tranquil voice. "We can beat up some fresh batter."

After lunch she would retire into my big armchair in the verandah. She would sit there for hours just fanning herself and looking out into the road. If a car stopped the armchair would groan as she strained forward to call me.

"Mrs. Dias, is it your husband you are expecting today?" I asked suddenly.

For a second she stared back at me as if she had received a shock. I had believed her to be incapable of any feeling but now I imagined I saw a flash of fear in her eyes. But it was only for a short moment. The next instant her face wore its usual composure.

"You are a clever girl," she announced as if I had made some startling discovery. "How did you guess it was my husband?"

"But does your husband live close by?" I had believed that there was only the jungle and road around us.

She stared out into the rain.

"My husband lives close to me always. There is no trouble for him to come here."

What a queer business! I thought.

"What do you mean he stays close to you, Mrs. Dias? Does he always follow you wherever you go?"

"Yes," she said flatly.

I tried to think it all out. If he was so devoted to her why did they live apart? Mrs. Dias smiled her slow smile and stroked my arm.

"You do not mind him coming here do you, Miss Edirisinghe? I promise you that we will not disturb you in any way."

"No, no, I do not mind. Please do not think that," I pleaded.

She sat down and started to clean the cutlery on the table. She had forgotten the flowers for her room. I looked at her curiously. Though she looked cool and unruffled I felt she was uncomfortable inside. She would take up a spoon, clean it halfway, and put it down again as if she found it impossible to concentrate.

"You must now look upon this place as your home. You must never again ask my permission to invite guests, Mrs. Dias," I said impulsively.

She looked at me gravely.

"Thank you, my dear, but I cannot do that. If I try to look upon it as my home, my husband will take advantage of it. He would begin to look upon it as his home too and that would be very awkward and uncomfortable for you. No, my dear, this is a nice place and I am very happy here but I must never make it my home."

Suddenly I was touched to the heart. Poor old soul, I thought. In spite of her unruffled attitude she was human with very human problems. All the time I believed her to be a mechanical robot she must have been fond of me in her silent way. But was her husband the monster she made him out to be? Looking at her it was hard to imagine that anybody, even a man, could get past that hard surface and break her heart. I had thought that she could have put up with anything. Apparently I was wrong again.

I did not ask Mrs. Dias any more questions. I felt she would not have answered them if I had. But I thought about what she had said to me. Coming from any other person it would not have been so sad. But Mrs. Dias had been so passive, so incapable of any feeling, that those few words coming out in that low voice sounded not only sad but tragic. It seemed as if Mrs. Dias in her own way had appealed for help.

"If I let my husband feel at home I would have to leave you."

Perhaps he had lived off her. Instead of providing her with a home he must be following her around trying to push himself into whatever temporary haven she found. Perhaps he was a hopeless drunkard, or a gambler. Or maybe even a woman-chaser though the last seemed a little ludicrous for a husband of

Mrs. Dias. Suddenly I giggled. Maybe that could be the truth. Certainly it was not impossible as I had thought. Maybe the husband of Mrs. Dias had nothing to do but to turn to another woman for consolation?

After lunch Mrs. Dias retired to her customary armchair. I retired to my room for a short nap. When I awoke three hours later it was dark and raining. Startled I leapt out of bed. Why hadn't Mrs. Dias called me as usual? Three hours! She had allowed me to sleep for three hours when customers may have called. I put on a housecoat and rushed outside.

The groceries were on the kitchen table. Twice a week I had them delivered from Peradeniya*. The boy must have come when I was asleep. I felt annoyed. Where on earth was old Mrs. Dias? Why hadn't she called me when the boy came? She knew I always checked the groceries before accepting them. Now owing to her laziness I may have lost half the goods.

Because I was angry I did not call her for tea. When the kettle of water was boiling, I prepared tea and poured myself a cup and went round to the front verandah. But Mrs. Dias was not there. The armchair was empty. Then I heard voices coming from her room. There was her dull flat voice and then a deep man's voice. Suddenly I remembered. Of course, Mrs. Dias' husband must have come!

I retraced my steps back to the kitchen. Now I knew why Mrs. Dias hadn't woken me up. I stood debating what to do. Then I made a fresh pot of tea and placing two of my best cups on a tray I took it to Mrs. Dias' room. It would be a nice gesture, I thought, this offering of tea on my part. It would make the old lady very happy too. She would be sure then in her heart that I did not grudge my home to her visitors. Moreover I was more than a little curious to see him.

Mrs. Dias' room door was closed. I knocked softly and waited. Instantly the voices ceased and there was a silence. I rapped again.

"Mrs. Dias, I have brought you some tea," I called out.

But the silence continued inside. Then I heard a slow shuffle of footsteps and the door was pushed open a fraction. Mrs. Dias' head came round it with difficulty.

"I do not want any tea," she said calmly. "Thank you, my dear, but I do not want any tea today."

The way she stood guarding the door was odd. It was as if she did not want me to see the inside of the room.

"But what about your husband?" I asked in surprise. "Surely he would like a cup of tea?"

"No, thank you, dear," she said again in her flat final voice. "He never takes tea."

Then she closed the door in my face.

I carried the tray back to the kitchen. My hands shook as I set it again on the table. I felt as if Mrs. Dias had slapped me in the face. I wanted to go back and say that I had had enough of her. I wanted to shout and scream and tell her to leave my house. Then my temper cooled and I began to feel I should be more sensible.

Mrs. Dias was a fool. Now I knew why she was anxious to guard her precious husband from me. She was jealous of me. The whole situation was so ridiculous that I laughed. I would get my own back, I vowed. Somehow I would force her hand and make her introduce me to her visitor. Then I would have achieved the impossible. I would have taken off that bland, peaceful mask she wore and revealed the true Mrs. Dias. My anger was all gone. I felt exhilarated and happy. At last life was worthwhile. I had something to look forward to.

It was apparently very late when the visitor left for Mrs. Dias did not come out of her room till eight-thirty. A storm was in full force and, because of the loud claps of thunder, I could not hear him leave. Serves Mrs. Dias right, I thought viciously. If she had been nice to me, her husband need not have gone out into the wet night. I would have invited him to sleep here. Then I remembered that she had said clearly that she did not want to make him feel at home.

She was her normal passive self at dinner. She never referred to her visitor or the unfortunate incident of the closed door. It was as if the whole thing had been conjured up by my imagination. She chatted lightly about the rain.

"I do hope it won't keep on all night. But of course you have a good roof so it should not matter even if it does. Why, the last place that I was in it simply poured down and wet my bed. You have seen that faded patch on the bedspread? Well that was where it got wet. Oh dear, was I upset about it! It was such a lovely bedspread too."

"I do hope your husband did not get wet going home," I could not help saying.

She smiled gently. "My husband never gets wet."

It was on the tip of my tongue to ask bitterly whether her husband was made out of mackintosh material that he should be so rainproof. Then I realized that it would be a waste of breath. Mrs. Dias was so thick-skinned that even the prick of a needle would never have been felt.

Thereafter Mrs. Dias entertained her husband daily in her room at five o'clock. I could have set my clock by his punctuality. In that way he seemed very like Mrs. Dias.

I made it a point to eavesdrop through the thin wall of her room. I could hear their voices clearly though the words were very often blurred and unintelligible. I began to like the deep pleasant tone of his voice. There was something so steady and strong and masculine about it. Husband and wife seemed very happy together. I could not deny that, however much I wanted to.

Gradually Mr. Dias became an obsession with me. I would find myself wandering towards the garden when it drew near five o'clock. But I never saw him come into the house. I would come out of the kitchen when I heard him bid Mrs. Dias good night in the hall, but it was always too late. He seemed to have gone the moment the words left his mouth. It was evident that he was either a very shy man or that his wife's instructions about not disturbing me had made a very deep impression. Poor man! He must have been compelled to use the back door more than once to avoid me.

Now and then I would try to question Mrs. Dias about her husband, in what I believed was a subtle manner. Over lunch or when we were working in the kitchen I would turn the conversation to family life. I told her everything about my own family, about my mother who was dead, my father and two brothers. But it was like throwing myself against a stone wall. She listened but never spoke.

Sometimes at night I would lie in the darkness and make believe that the mysterious Mr. Dias was next door to his wife's room. He was a tall man, yes, and good-looking and gentle in manner. He had seen me in the garden, though I had not seen him, and he had fallen in love with me. He wanted to meet me but he had a conscience; he would always do the proper thing by his wife even though he was unhappy. He dared not speak to me.

The more I played with this picture, the more I liked it. I began to improve, enlarge on it, as the weeks went by and nothing happened to bring Mr. Dias to my presence. Sometimes when my imagination ran away with me I would compare my slim figure with that of corpulent Mrs. Dias and pity poor Mr. Dias.

Were it not for Mr. Dias I believe I would have soon got rid of Mrs. Dias. She seemed to turn duller and duller as the weeks went by. She was like a buffalo that wallows contentedly in the mud. Then the crisis occurred.

I met Mr. Dias.

The evening that it happened turned out to be one of the hottest on the calendar. I had had a tiring day for the road had been busy. I lost count of the cars that stopped near the gate. Mrs. Dias helped me count the money and put it away in the tin box I kept in the dining room. I knew her well enough now to be able to detect the slight variation of expression, or rather the feeling, that Mrs. Dias was upset over something. She moved placidly as ever, but somehow I knew the difference.

"Anything troubling you, Mrs. Dias?" I asked.

She raised mild brown eyes to mine.

"I was wondering dear, would you mind very much if my husband stayed overnight only this once? You see he has to go away for a few days and we will not be seeing each other for a week or so. We won't be any trouble I promise you."

My heart beat fast. At last the opportunity I had been waiting for. This time I would be firm and stand for no flimsy excuses of refusal.

"I do not mind at all, Mrs. Dias," I said warmly. "Please ask your husband to stay the night and we can all have dinner together."

"Please do not worry about dinner," she said quickly. "My husband never takes dinner."

"Come now, Mrs. Dias!" I said firmly. "Surely you do not expect me to believe that? Your husband must have some dinner with us. How can we expect him to go hungry?"

"But my husband will never eat it," she said stubbornly. "The food will only go to waste."

"Then let him sit at table while we eat," I cried recklessly. "For I would love to meet your husband."

You are not going to shut him away from me again, I

told myself. Oh no. This time you are not going to win.

"But you do understand," she said helplessly. "You cannot meet my husband and be happy again."

I had been right then. She was afraid that I would seduce her husband away from her.

"Why do you say that, Mrs. Dias? Surely your husband cannot annoy a landlady to that extent!"

"Miss Edirisinghe, you are young and do not understand the situation I am placed in. Please do not insist on seeing my husband."

"But I do insist," I said boldly. "Mrs. Dias I will be very angry if I cannot meet your husband. Surely we know each other well enough not to be afraid of what your husband may say to me. I promise you I will not be angry with him and that I will not drive you out of the house on account of it."

She moved to the window and gazed out at the bright sunshine. She stood there for a long time just staring. I moved close to her and placed my hand gently on her shoulder. The soft flesh quivered and it was all I could do to prevent my hand from withdrawing in repulsion.

"Dear Mrs. Dias, do not worry. I only want to meet him for your sake."

She turned and looked at me squarely. There was no resentment or fear on her face.

"Very well. As you are so anxious to meet him we will come to dinner. Please knock on the door when you want us to come."

I had won. But her indifference made it difficult to enjoy the victory. All that fuss and now it seemed she cared little whether I did, or did not, meet her husband.

But I soon ceased to worry about Mrs. Dias. I decided the dinner would be yellow rice and chicken curry in honour of the occasion. I spared no pain over the cooking. Surely when Mr. Dias smelt the succulent aroma of that chicken he would eat? Strange to say Mrs. Dias did not offer to help as usual. She retired to her room and did not come out all evening.

I do not know what prompted me to take such care over what I should wear that evening. Finally I decided on a pale pink georgette saree that had been in mothballs since I was eighteen, twenty years ago. But tonight I did not think it looked too frivolous. It was not only the very young that were privileged to wear pink.

I brushed out my short hair and added a pair of gold

earrings. Poor Mrs. Dias. I must put on a show for her sake. I must make her feel that everything was going to turn out all right.

As usual I did not see Mr. Dias come but I soon heard his voice inside the room. They were both talking and by the sound of the voices they seemed to be having an argument. That is Mr. Dias' voice was raised while hers remained flat. I frowned. I hoped Mrs. Dias was not trying to persuade him to be without dinner. One never knew what went on behind that broad smooth manner of hers.

At eight-thirty I knocked sharply on the door. Instantly the voices ceased and I heard her slow heavy footsteps cross the floor. The door opened a little.

"Dinner is ready," I announced brightly.

Mrs. Dias slowly pushed the door wide open. Her eyes were on my face and though I looked back at her I could see nothing but the faintest trace of perspiration on her brow.

It was warm, for the windows were closed. How absurd to close the windows when it was so hot! The room looked the same. Nothing had changed since Mrs. Dias moved in two months ago. There were the same cheap bric-a-brac on the table, the same vase of flowers, the brown curtains at the windows. The room was all there in its stolid strength. I looked around carefully. But where was Mr. Dias?

"He is over near the bed," said Mrs. Dias.

I looked at the empty space around the bed with the purple-satin cover, and wondered whether it was Mrs. Dias or I who had gone mad.

"He is there, dear," she insisted. "See now he is smiling at you. Don't be shy, Carl. Come and shake hands with Miss Edirisinghe."

"Mrs. Dias," I said slowly. "Mrs. Dias are you feeling all right?"

Mrs. Dias looked back at me. The perspiration was clearly visible now on her forehead and she looked sad. It was queer to see Mrs. Dias looking so sad. I had believed her to be incapable of emotion.

"I warned you, Miss Edirisinghe, that there would be trouble if you tried to see my husband. Poor man! He died eleven years ago and from that day he has never known a stable home. People do not like to have him in the house and I cannot keep him a secret for sooner or later they always find out. They

become terrified when they discover the truth. They hold *pirith**
ceremonies and tie charms to exorcize the presence of my Carl.
As if he were a devil or an evil spirit! My poor gentle Carl who
only comes to see me. YOU are not afraid of my husband, are
you, dear? See, he is harmless as a baby. Though you cannot see
him he is there waiting silently."

I jerked back towards the door. If I did not move fast
Mrs. Dias might kill me. Fool that I was not to have realized that
there was insanity under my own roof. Underneath that terrible
calm, Mrs. Dias was insane.

Mrs. Dias smiled at me sadly. Then she wandered towards the bed.

"Carl, we will have to leave this house too. She is afraid
of you, Carl. See how she is running away from you even now.
Tell her not to be afraid, Carl!"

She was stark raving mad. The thing to do was to remain
calm and then go for help without her knowing it. I fixed a smile
on my face and continued to move towards the door. Then a
deep gentle voice spoke to me from the empty bed.

* **Colombo:** capital of Sri Lanka
* **Kandy:** city in central Sri Lanka
* **hot hoppers:** a food similar to pancakes
* **string-hoppers:** very thin noodles
* **mulligatawny:** highly seasoned curry soup
* **saree:** garment consisting of a long piece of cloth worn draped around the body; worn primarily by Hindu women (also spelled **sari**)

* **konde:** hair piled at the back of the head in a bun or knot
* **Peradeniya:** university town near Kandy
* **pirith:** a collection of Buddhist hymns and sermons, read publicly to ward off evil

Pablo Tamayo

NAOMI SHIHAB NYE

ablo Tamayo is moving today, to stay with his brother-in-law on Nueces Street till he can find another house. "Don't worry so much," he told me over the fence. "I'm a beat-up man, my wife is an old lady, I always told you the roof was gonna fall."

That's wrong. He never mentioned the roof. He used to call on the telephone and say in a gruff voice, "Who's there?" as if I'd called him. When I stuttered, he'd laugh and say, "This is me, I'm standing on your roof," but he never mentioned falling.

I want to give him eggs, a flannel shirt. I want to tell him this neighborhood will be a vacuum without him. To go back to the beginning, make a catalog of his utterances since the day we met over the bamboo that divides our yards. I was standing on a ladder with clippers, trying to tell the bamboo who was boss. In the next yard he stooped over a frizzy dog, murmuring Spanish consolations. He looked like he might once have been a wrestler. "So," he said, looking up. "You're pretty tall, I guess." I told him I was his new neighbor and he said he was my old one. He pointed, "Look at how I put this eyeball back in my dog."

Once his dog had a fight with a German shepherd. Pablo came running to find the eyeball dangling on its string. He called a doctor, the doctor said twenty dollars at least. "So I do it myself.

Good job, no?" The eye was now glassy white. It looked like it had been put in backwards. "My dog goes with me to Junior's Lounge," he said, giggling. You don't expect giggles from a man with tattoos. He told me Welcome to the Neighborhood, it's a Nice Neighborhood, I been here Forty, you know, Years. Throwing his head back when he spoke, like somebody proud and practiced, or kicking up dust, looking down like a kid, a brand-new kid.

Later I found myself wondering about him. What made this man act so happy? His house tilted, his wife had no teeth. We invited them for dinner, but they wouldn't come. "She don't like to chew without teeth in public." His car had not run in twenty weeks. Where was his history, what was his life?

"I was born in Mexico, like half the people in this town. They get born, they go north. Like birds or something." One night he showed me their wedding pictures. Such devastating changes the years make! From a shining silken couple, a future of roses, to a house of orange crates and dead newspapers, a shuffling duet of slippers and beans. "I love another girl first, her daddy was rich. He told her never marry a baker." His face goes dark for a moment. "Sometimes I still think of that. There was a rooster who rode on my shoulder but one day he changed, you know, he bit me on the leg." When Pablo speaks of the village in the mountains south of Monterrey, he stops smiling, as if those memories are a cathedral which can only be entered with a sober face.

The next day I ask him when he bought his house. "Aw, I never did. They wanted me to, in 1939. But I didn't like to pay so much money all at once, so I just keep payin' forty dollars a month till now." I want to shake him. Who is his landlord? "A bad, bad man. Once I had a good man but they change over the years. This guy, he won't fix the pipe, he won't paint the outside. I want to paint it, but he won't let me. What color do you think I could paint it?"

We stand back to examine the peeling boards.

"Beige."

Three days later he knocks at my door. "I just want to ask you. Is that the color of coffee with milk in it?"

His wife speaks no English and loves to wash. She wears a faded apron, veteran of a thousand washtubs. I can imagine her getting up in the mornings and going straight to her sewing machine. In a cage outside her back door lives a featherless bird named "Pobrecito." Pablo found it on Sweet Street, hobbling. She feeds it scraps of melon and bread.

Around her telephone she has pinned an arc of plastic lilies, postcards of saints, a rosary of black beads. Who is she hoping will call? If Jesus were to manifest for her in modern ways—*Buenas dias!** she would say. *Mi casita, mi perrito, mi Pobrecito*, mi Jesús.* I have a garage sale and she buys my battered hiking boots. Where is she planning to go?

After much prodding, Pablo tells me they have three children. Two are in their fifties, live in Houston or somewhere. "Naw, I don't see them, they don't see me." One is twenty. Pablo and his wife are more than seventy so that means she had the boy when she was fifty, at least. I ask him about this and he says he guesses it's true. Months later I hear another story from the widow down the street. The twenty-year-old is a grandson. She says, "Pablo lies."

When the boy comes home he turns on rock-and-roll so loud the candles quiver on our piano. His hair is longer than my hair. Pablo says, "He had bad luck. Got married too young, seventeen, something like that, to a girl born north of the border. That means she's lazy. It's true. If a Mexican is born north of the border, her husband will walk the road of tears. So they broke up. Bad luck."

Months later, after numerous references to the road of tears, I ask Pablo for details. You mean to tell me all the smooth-faced innocent-hearted Mexican girls in local high schools are going to have husbands who walk the road of tears? C'mon Pablo, find your way out of that one. He looks at me, puzzled. And then his face cracks into its goofy grin. "I got it," he says. "You get a boat."

He asks what I do, why I'm always in this house chattering away on my typing machine. "I write things down," I say.

"Like what things?"

"Like little things that happen."

He looks around, shrugs. "I don't see nothin' happenin'." Then he goes indoors to make me a perfect pie. Pablo understands pie crust, for him poetry is the fluted edge of dough. And Pablo is the only one who will ever understand the delicate grammar of the engine of his car. There was no fuel pump in the city, he said dramatically, which would fit it. So he was building a contraption of wire and soup cans, like a child's telephone. He was going to communicate with his car.

One day, after nearly a month of tinkering, I heard the engine cough, choke, exhale a huge sigh. And there was Pablo passing my house, waving madly, his one-eyed dog perched in the back window. Ten minutes later he was back. There was a problem—the car could only go as far as the amount of gas the can would hold. But it *worked* now. That was the important thing, it worked. One night I dreamed that wings sprouted where the dented door handles were and Pablo went flying over the city, sending down lines of symbolic verse.

He said he would get another "Alamo seed" so I could have a tree like the one in his yard. He said he was tired of the mud out back, he had this plan for grass. "I used to drink more beers," he said, "than any man with a mouth." That was when he worked at the hotel, when he came home with cinnamon in his cuffs. Some days now he still journeyed out to work, dressed in a square white baker's shirt, to cafeterias or hospitals to "fill in" for someone's absence. "I made thirty-five dozen doughnuts today," he'd say, folding his craggy hands, shaking his head. "I don't wanna be like the man who killed himself in your bathroom." This was news to me. *What man?*

Then Pablo looked worried, he'd slipped, he'd said too much. "Aw, come on, I was joking, let's go hammer the fence, aye-yi-yi." He got shy sometimes, his words blurred. *What man?* And he told me his name. Howard Riley. Spoken slowly, Howard Ri-ley, as if the name had grown longer than Pablo's head.

"He was an old man, kinda old, you know, oh what the hell, everybody's old. You're kinda old. He was old a little sooner than I was. He used to hit a golf ball in the yard, that end, this end, that end, this end. I hear this little tick, you know, like the clock, the little sound it made. But one day he went in your bathroom and shot his own head. Pow! (Finger to head.) I was at the bank. I came home with ten dollars, and my wife, she said, Howard's dead. In Spanish, you know. So I went over to see him and he was gone already. They came in a car and took him. I just went to the bank! I used to think of him at night when the nuts fell on the roof. Tick, tick, tick."

"Why did he do it?"

A shrug. "I dunno. He was tired. He had nothin' else to do." Pablo stared down at his two big feet. "So let's go hammer the fence, I get the hammer, you get the nails."

Months later, on the same day I was watching him busy

at work in his yard at 7:00 a.m., wearing a blue-and-white checkered jockey cap, dragging a tin pail of cilantro from one mud-crease to the next, that day his faceless landlord appeared and told him they had two weeks to get gone. After forty-eight years, two weeks. Pablo came to me with the same expression my father had on the day he had to fire twelve lifetime printers from his newspaper because they were being replaced by computers.

"We gotta move."

The little dog was running in circles, sniffing the ground. Another fall, pecans splitting their dull-green pods in the grass. A pumpkin pie still warm in my hands. How many pies had Pablo given us? Maybe a hundred, maybe more. Lots of times we gave them away. We don't like pie too much. But we'd keep them out on the table awhile, on a small pedestal, like a shrine.

"This one's good."

He'd always say it. "This one's good." Forget any other one. Pablo in the yard with a ragged tea towel on his arm, hands outstretched.

"What do you mean, move?"

His landlord wanted to build an office. I was yelling about zoning while his wife unpinned the rosary from its wall, felt the cool black beads move again in her fingers. "You know, he might make a parking lot here where the Alamo tree is." This year the tree had eighteen leaves. From that seed Pablo found in the gutter. We joked so much when it came up, ugly stick. Not one leaf for months. Then he put small twigs around it like a barricade, tied them with string, little red flags, and it started doing things. His voodoo tree. Smack in the center of the yard.

I wanted to meet this damn landlord immediately. Where had he gone? What kind of office? With filing cabinets and Dictaphones and a secretary's shiny legs? Obviously they wouldn't fit in this tilt-a-whirl little house, they'd flatten it out, 'doze it under. Pablo's crooked stove. The ancient valentine heart tacked to the porch. From whom to whom? Gruff voice. "Me to the lady."

He stood there in his yard which was slipping out from under him, he stood there with his hips cocked, plaid shirt half-buttoned, his hair still full on his head, and said, "I wanna tell you somethin'." That always meant, come a little closer, put down your groceries. "You know this world we got here?" he motioned with his arms. "Lemme tell you, this world don't love us. It don't think about us or pray for us or miss us, you know what I mean? That's what I learned when my father died. I was a young man. I got up the next day and went outside, feelin' sick, my face still fat from cryin'. And there was the sky. Lookin' just the same. Dead or alive, it don't matter. Still the sky. So then I started lookin' around and there was still the flowers, still the bugs, I mean *the bugs*, who cares about bugs? My father was dead and the world didn't miss him. The world didn't know his name! Ventura—Morales—Tamayo—but I *knew* it. And I say to myself, That's all we got! I know it, the barber know it, so what? This don't make me feel more bad, you know, it make me feel—better. Aw, I dunno, I gotta go find a box."

Hours later he's coming down Sheridan Street pushing a box in front of him, a giant box, like the boxes washing machines come in. He's done this before. I never knew what he did with those boxes. They went in the door and disappeared. He doesn't have a fireplace. Inside his wife is taking down the sweaters. They have the smell of sunlight in them. She's had them out on those poles and ropes so many times they're a little confused today. Now they're going someplace else. She's shufflin' around and he's shufflin' around, taking down calendars, rolling up the years. God knows where the boy is when they need him. Pablo probably rolls up his "Boogie Brothers" poster without even reading it.

Once he said, "When you die, you die."

"Oh yeah? That's very interesting."

Then we were laughing ridiculously on our two sides of the fence.

Can I translate this great philosophy so it applies to now? "When you move, you move." Simple. Throw up the hands. Still we're very upset in our house. The sky doesn't know it, but we know it. The news comes on the television. I go out back. There is no other news.

* **Buenas dias:** "Good day"
* **Mi casita, mi perrito, mi Pobrecito...:** my little house, my dear little dog; Pobrecito (poor little one) is the name of the bird

Appearances

J.M. SMALL

What passes for truth is often only myth: All brides are beautiful; crime doesn't pay; lawyers are wealthy.

Howard Jessup was a lawyer and he was far from wealthy. Only his partner, his bank and his accountant knew how far he was from the stereotype of the rich, three-piece-suited, confident professional of the myth.

Howard Jessup was an intelligent man, but he was not smart. Greed had taken him down the shady path of risk ventures, commodity markets, MURBs*, real estate and restaurant franchises. At the end of the path there loomed, not the skiing chalet in Switzerland and the white beaches of Maui, but the terrifying portals of the bankruptcy trustee's office.

A shudder passed through his body. His father had built a stable and conservative law firm by stable and conservative means. His father's death left Jessup senior partner and he wallowed in the new-found freedom and independence.

But after five years, the firm and its assets were in serious financial jeopardy, and getting there had not been nearly as much fun as Howard had supposed. Now the accountant was giving the same advice given so often by his father: Get rid of the dead wood; tighten your belt; trim the sails; get back on firm footing. The confusion of metaphors aside, Jessup knew it was advice he should—he must—take.

Belt-tightening was the first item on the fiscal agenda. The firm's heavily-mortgaged condominium was sold, at a slight loss. The expense vouchers for staff lawyers' lunches and travel were questioned and sometimes rejected or reduced. Leased deluxe foreign cars were traded in on more modest vehicles. The firm, briefly known for its open-handed policies and its lawyers who always picked up the tab, quickly became spartan.

Still, Howard Jessup was worried. Some of the debts had been paid off and many of the expenses trimmed. There was still a vast shortfall caused by some of his more disastrous forays into the financial world. The corporate belt was tight, its sails were trimmed, the footing was not yet quite firm, but at least it was no longer on a foundation of quicksand. The time had come to burn the dead wood.

Three junior lawyers felt the flames first. Their files could easily be distributed among Jessup, his partner Reg Nicholai, and the two remaining staff lawyers.

Falling axes have a way of making people work harder. Clerical and secretarial employees, working feverishly to protect their jobs in this sudden new climate of industriousness, found they had time on their hands. Idle hands had no place in the re-born Jessup & Nicholai offices. Four office staff may even now be pacing the pavement remembering Black Friday, the day four terminating letters appeared with their pay cheques.

Ellen Schmidt was the only person believed to be truly safe, perhaps because Howard Jessup feared her. Miss Schmidt (as she was always known) had worked for Jessup's father from the day he had begun his practice until his death. Her age was a subject of speculation and it was believed she was somewhere over seventy; no one was ever sure, or would dare to ask.

She had drunk a glass of champagne with Jessup Sr. at the birth of his son, comforted her employer when his wife died young, and bullied young Howard through law school and articles.

Miss Schmidt was universally respected, though generally feared. Forty years in the same job had made her rigid in her ways and stern with those who did not subscribe to her creed. That creed had made her invaluable to the senior Mr. Jessup. Her whole being was directed to doing what was best for the firm.

Ellen Schmidt had viewed Jessup's fiscal adventures with alarm and disgust. She saw a thirty-five-year-old man behaving childishly and irresponsibly. Her suggestions for restraint had been greeted with a curt rebuke and she had realized that young Howard would not see reason. For the good of the firm, and within her limited real power, she maintained the illusion that all was well at Jessup & Nicholai, and succeeded.

"Miss Schmidt. Could I see you in my office?" said Howard.

"Yes, sir. I'll just get my book." The "sir" came naturally to Miss Schmidt's lips, but Howard always thought he detected a touch of sarcasm, a private sneer.

With Howard in safety behind his broad desk and Miss Schmidt poised in a client chair with her pencil raised above the steno pad, Howard began.

"We won't have dictation just yet, Miss Schmidt. There are a few matters I'd like to discuss with you."

Drops of nervous sweat trickled down his scalp and came to rest in his sideburns. He launched into his prepared speech under the benign gaze of this frightening woman. He told her that the firm, as she must know, had some financial difficulties. Steps had been taken to reduce the overhead and to streamline the operation. Success was in sight, but what was needed now was the whole-hearted co-operation of everyone in the firm to work through the minor setback.

Behind that impassive exterior, was she laughing at him? Did she long to point a finger and say, "I told you so"? Why didn't she say anything? He hoped she would not think it odd that he was using his pristine handkerchief to blot his hairline in the cool office.

He said that, for the good of the firm, ways must be found to deal with unnecessary expenses, to begin a cautious program of modernization, to work towards the day when Jessup & Nicholai would once again be the solid, conservative firm it had been when his father lived. He appealed to her. He knew that Miss Schmidt, a long-time and valued employee, could be counted on to do what was right, what was best for the firm.

Ellen Schmidt softened to the young man before her. He was asking for her help at last and it was causing him a great deal of anxiety to do so. She would find a way; it was the least she could do. Her face and voice betrayed nothing of this; she merely nodded and assured Jessup she would give the matter serious thought.

Howard Jessup decided against giving dictation that morning. He was too exhausted. Miss Schmidt returned to her desk. Howard poured a stiff drink and called in Reg Nicholai.

"God, she really put you through the wringer. You look terrible!" said Nicholai, pouring himself a double.

"Thank you for those heartening words," said Jessup. "I'd imagined a scene or a lecture, but she was quite calm."

"And did you get it? Did it work?" demanded Nicholai.

"Yes. Or at least I think it worked. I played up her famous for-the-good-of-the-firm line and I believe she took the bait. If I'm right, she'll hand in her resignation before the week's out.

"My late father's generosity landed us with the highest-paid secretary in the city. Hell, if the lawyers found out she was making more than they are, we'd have a revolt! I'm quite looking forward to the day when I see the end of Miss Ellen Schmidt and can replace her with someone unthreatening, and at a third of the salary we pay the Dragon Lady. Let's go get an expense account lunch for a change, just to celebrate."

Celebration was premature. While Howard Jessup and Reg Nicholai enjoyed a long, expensive and quite liquid lunch, Miss Schmidt took her usual forty-five minutes in the lunch-room. From long habit, she normally spent her lunch break doing homework or studying whatever subject she was taking that term at night school.

That day, she ate her sandwich and drank her tea without thinking about school. Her thoughts were all on her campaign to salvage the firm. She considered extending a loan to the mis-guided boys (she always called them "the boys" in her mind). With a generous salary and modest needs, she had amassed a substantial sum over the years, enough for a very comfortable retirement at some vague future date.

She rejected the idea, wrongly believing that Jessup would never accept the money. Further belt-tightening could be undertaken. That saucy, young secretary who worked for Mr. Nicholai could be let go. She produced so little work for a secre-tary, there would be no problem distributing it around the office. The two remaining staff lawyers and the secretary they shared should stay; the lawyers both worked hard and had partnership potential. A major infusion of capital was called for, and lots of hard work. At no time did Miss Schmidt even consider the possi-bility of her own retirement as a money-saving option.

The week went by and no letter of resignation appeared on Howard Jessup's desk. His confidence in his persuasive powers suffered a severe blow and Reg teased him in his light, bantering way. Reg's tone changed on Friday when his secretary came to him in tears, demanding an explanation of the pink slip she waved. Miss Schmidt did have authority to hire and fire, but she had gone too far.

Nicholai raved at her in the open office. He called her names, but she sat unmoved, determined to do what was best for the firm. In the end, Nicholai was amazed to find himself apologizing to her and then helping the blubbering Stephanie gather her possessions for the final trip from the office. With Stephanie in the same office, the affair had been easy to manage. It threatened to become very expensive now.

Sunday morning, very early, the police phoned Howard Jessup. The car was leased in the firm name and Jessup was the first to learn of the traffic death of his partner. Shocked and over-whelmed by the latest tragedy, Howard drove slowly to the scene. The familiar car was a modern sculpture in blackened metal, still hot from the fire, on the road below the cliffs. Reg's body was unrecognizable.

The next day, the policeman came. Positive identification would be made from the dental records. Reg had been visiting Stephanie and left for his own apartment after an argument, ap-parently concerning Stephanie's dismissal from the firm. The policeman was gentle, a good listener.

Howard was later surprised to recall how much informa-tion he had volunteered—all about the money problems, Reg's drinking, the scene at the office on Friday, Reg's terrible driving, his worry about Stephanie. The policeman just nodded and kept on writing, rather like Miss Schmidt taking dictation. Howard idly wondered if the policeman would improve his grammar as Miss Schmidt always did.

The policeman and other, more senior men came back several times. After the funeral, and when the shock had worn off, Howard was less forthcoming. He was a busy man and there was a great deal of work to be done. The police officers went away and Jessup did, indeed, work.

He discovered that his partner had been very sloppy, legally, with his files. Jessup and Miss Schmidt worked long hours to clean up the mess and to contact clients and issue writs before limitation dates passed. He was glad then that she had not retired and began to appreciate for the first time what a valuable member of the firm Ellen Schmidt was.

The police were concerned. Reg Nicholai had been drinking—there was no question about that—but his blood alcohol level was below the legal limit. The blackened pile that had been his car offered little evidence. But there was a feeling, an intuition, that all was not as it appeared. Nothing could be proved, it was only a vague suspicion.

The coroner, already annoyed with the delay caused by the police adjournment, ruled eventually as he had originally planned to rule: death by accident, with a warning against drinking and driving, and a blast at the city for inadequate safety retainers along the cliff road. The case was closed.

Howard Jessup stared at the cheque. Two hundred thousand dollars, payable to the firm. He looked to Miss Schmidt for enlightenment. It was the insurance payment on Mr. Nicholai's life. There had always been partnership insurance, or was he not aware of that? Miss Schmidt took the cheque off to the bookkeeper. Jessup & Company was on the way back up.

The office seemed oppressively warm to Howard. He was sweating again. No one had asked Miss Schmidt any questions about Reg's accident, there was no need. Even if they had, she was old and fragile-looking and would not have spoken of her life outside of the office. It was only to Jessup's father that she'd spoken of the private Ellen Schmidt, and Jessup Sr. had mentioned it to his son.

He remembered now. She took courses in the evenings on all kinds of subjects—conversational French, cake decorating, comparative religion, psychology—and once, auto mechanics.

Howard remembered that frail old Miss Schmidt had fixed the brakes on his father's car years ago when he was having trouble with them. She had done a very professional job. He assumed she would have equal competence with steering, for the good of the firm.

* **MURBs:** Multiple Unit Rental Buildings

The Collection

TERRENCE HEATH

i 'll give you three hockey players for no. 3 of the animals.

no.

why not? what's so hot about a triceratop anyhow?

you ever see no. 3 before? i know a boy's got all the sports cards. but i don't know anyone with this card.

ah, lots of kids have it.

i never seen it.

look, i'll give you this destroyer and pt boat too.

they're your doubles. i only got one of these. nobody else's ever got it and you want to give me your lousy doubles.

o.k. i'll give you all the sports cards i got.

is it alla them?

no, but almost. i'll give you my doubles too. there's lots there you don't have.

well. all for this no. 3? why you want this card so bad?

i got all the animals but that one.

let's see.

see. 1, 2, 4, 5, alla them.

yah. what if there's only one of these ever made?

they wouldn't do that. there's lotsa them.

yah? well, i want to keep it.

you haven't even got all the other animals. what you goin to do with it anyway?

i dunno. just keep it.

Wilma

WILMA RUDOLPH

So it's 1956, and I'm a fifteen-year-old high school sophomore, and my life has never been better. I couldn't remember being happier. School was fun then. I remember the television show "American Bandstand" was very big with the kids, and once a week somebody would come into the school with a bunch of records and we'd have our own "American Bandstand" show after school. They would give out records to kids who won dance contests doing the latest dances, and I even won a couple myself. All the girls were wearing long, tight skirts, the ones that ended just below the knees, and bobby socks and padded bras. They wore chains around their necks with their boyfriends' rings on them, and if you were going steady with an athlete, the girl wore the guy's letter sweaters or his team jacket. Little Richard* was big, and Chuck Berry* was big, but truthfully, Elvis Presley* had no effect whatsoever. Burt High School was all black, and we just didn't have any kids in the school who identified with Elvis Presley. The black kids sort of knew that he was just a white guy singing black music, but no black kids had motorcycles or leather jackets, probably because they didn't have the money to buy them.

We had all sorts of little social groups in the school, but none that could be described as being like white greasers. One group was the dressers, the kids who came from fairly affluent homes and showed it off by wearing the best clothes all the time, even to the point where some of the guys in this group came to school wearing suits and ties. The next group was the regulars, the kids who were looked upon as being regular kids, nothing special, just everyday happy kids. Athletes were another group and they usually stuck with other athletes. The funniest group was the "process" guys. They would go to barber shops and get their hair straightened, and everybody would talk about how the barbers used lye to straighten out their hair. Then they would slick back the straightened hair, and this slick look became known as the "Process Look." The guys thought it gave them a worldly image, the image of being real slick dudes who hung around in nightclubs and travelled with the fastest company. But most of them did just the opposite; they travelled with other process guys only.

My whole life at the time revolved around basketball and my family. Robert was my boyfriend; we went out on dates, and when there was nothing else to do, we'd all go hang out at the local teenage club. Life seemed so uncomplicated, and happy, then.

As soon as the basketball season ended, I had my track stuff on, and I was running. There was a kid in school everybody called "Sundown"; the reason he was called that was because he was so black. His real name was Edward. Anyway, he and I used to skip out of classes almost every day, and we'd sneak off across the street to the municipal stadium, and we'd throw our books over the big wall that surrounded the stadium, then we'd climb the fence and run over to the track and do some running. If we heard any strange sounds, like somebody was coming, we'd run underneath the stands and hide.

Sometimes, when the college track team from Austin Peay College was using the stadium, the place would be filled with these white guys practising. "Sundown" and I would show up out of the clear blue sky, and they would look, and sort of blink and then go back about their business. The coach of the college team, this white guy, sort of knew that I was skipping out of classes to practise running; he would give me this little wink, like he knew what was going on but like he also had a little bit of admiration for me because I was so in love with running. Whenever he talked to his team, I would sort of hang around on the fringes and listen, hoping to pick up a pointer or two for free.

I think he noticed that, too, and when he saw me sort of hanging around, it always seemed he would start talking a little louder than before.

That taste of winning I had gotten the year before never left me. I was more serious about track now, thinking deep down inside that maybe I had a future in the sport if I tried hard enough. So I thought nothing of cutting classes and going out to run. But one day I got a call to report to the principal's office. I went in, and he said, "Wilma, all of us here know just how important running track is to you. We all know it, and we are all hoping that you become a big success at it. But you can't keep cutting classes and going out to run." I was, well, mortified; the principal had found me out. He finally said that if I continued cutting classes, he would have to tell my father, and I knew what that meant. So I stopped. Even so, I was the first girl out there at practice and the last one to leave, I loved it so. We had some more of those playday-type meets early that season, and I kept on winning all the races I was in. I felt unbeatable.

Then came the big meet at Tuskegee, Alabama. It was the big meet of the year. Girls from all over the South were invited down there to run, and the competition was the best for high school kids. It was a whole weekend type of thing, and they had dances and other things planned for the kids when they weren't out running. Coach Gray was going to drive us all down there to Tuskegee Institute, where the meet was held, and I remember we brought our very best dresses. We all piled into his car until there wasn't an inch of empty space in that car. Mrs. Allison, my old teacher, came with us; she was going to chaperone us at the big dance after the meet.

All the way down to Alabama, we talked and laughed and had a good time, and Coach Gray would tell us how tough the competition was going to be, especially the girls from Atlanta, Georgia, because they had a lot of black schools down there, and they had these track programs that ran the whole year because of the warm weather. When we got there, all of us were overwhelmed, because that was the first college campus any of us ever saw. We stayed in this big dorm, and I remember just before the first competition, I started getting this nervous feeling that would stay with me for the rest of my running career. Every time before a race, I would get it, this horrible feeling in the pit of my stomach, a combination of nerves and not eating.

When we got to the track, these girls from Georgia really looked like runners, but I paid them no mind because, well, I was a little cocky. I did think I could wipe them out because, after all, I had won every single race I had ever been in up to that point. So what happens? I got wiped out. It was the absolute worst experience of my life. I did not win a single race I ran in, nor did I qualify for anything. I was totally crushed. The girls from Georgia won everything. It was the first time I had ever tasted defeat in track, and it left me a total wreck. I was so despondent that I refused to go to any of the activities that were planned, including the big dance. I can't remember ever being so totally crushed by anything.

On the ride back, I sat in the car and didn't say a word to anybody, I just thought to myself about how much work was ahead of me and how I would like nothing better in the whole world than to come back to Tuskegee the next year and win everything. When I got home, my father knew immediately what had happened, and he didn't say anything. Every time I used to come home after a meet, I would rush into the house all excited and bubble over with, "I won...I won." This time I didn't say a word. I just walked in quietly, nodded to my father who was sitting there, and went into my room and unpacked.

After so many easy victories, using natural ability alone, I got a false sense of being unbeatable. But losing to those girls from Georgia, who knew every trick in the book, that was sobering. It brought me back down to earth, and it made me realize that I couldn't do it on natural ability alone, that there was more to track than just running fast. I also realized it was going to test me as a person—could I come back and win again after being so totally crushed by a defeat?

When I went back to school, I knew I couldn't continue to cut classes to practise or else I'd be in big trouble. So I would fake sickness, tell the teacher that I didn't feel well and could I please go home? They would let me go, and then I would go over to the track and run. When that stopped working, when they realized that I looked pretty good for being sick all the time, I simply asked them point-blank, "Look, could I cut this class today and go out and run?" Believe it or not, a lot of teachers said, "Okay, Wilma, go, but don't tell anybody."

I ran and ran and ran every day, and I acquired this sense of determination, this sense of spirit that I would never,

never give up, no matter what else happened. That day at Tuskegee had a tremendous effect on me inside. That's all I ever thought about. Some days I just wanted to go out and die. I just moped around and felt sorry for myself. Other days I'd go out to the track with fire in my eyes, and imagine myself back at Tuskegee, beating them all. Losing as badly as I did had an impact on my personality. Winning all the time in track had given me confidence; I felt like a winner. But I didn't feel like a winner any more after Tuskegee. My confidence was shattered and I was thinking the only way I could put it all together was to get back the next year and wipe them all out.

But looking back on it all, I realized somewhere along the line that to think that way wasn't necessarily right, that it was kind of extreme. I learned a very big lesson for the rest of my life as well. The lesson was, winning is great, sure, but if you are really going to do something in life, the secret is learning how to lose. Nobody goes undefeated all the time. If you can pick up after a crushing defeat, and go on to win again, you are going to be a champion someday. But if losing destroys you, it's all over. You'll never be able to put it all back together again.

I did, almost right away. There were more playdays scheduled, and I won all the rest of the races I was in the rest of that season. But I never forgot Tuskegee. In fact, I was thinking that anybody who saw me lose so badly at the meet would write me off immediately. I was wrong. One day, right after the track season ended that year, Coach Gray came over to me and he said, "Wilma, Ed Temple, the referee who is the women's track coach at Tennessee State, is going to be coming down to Clarksville to talk with your mother and father."

"What about?" I asked.

"Wilma," he said, "I think he wants you to spend the summer with him at the college, learning the techniques of running."

* **Little Richard, Chuck Berry, Elvis Presley:** rock 'n' roll singers who first achieved popularity in the 1950s and 1960s

Sonata for Harp
And Bicycle

JOAN AIKEN

"**N**o one is allowed to remain in the building after five p.m.," Mr. Manaby told his new assistant, showing him into the little room that was like the inside of an egg carton.

"Why not?"

"Directorial policy," said Mr. Manaby. But that was not the real reason.

Gaunt and sooty, Grimes Buildings lurched up the side of a hill towards Clerkenwell. Every little office within its dim and crumbling exterior owned one tiny crumb of light—such was the proud boast of the architect—but towards evening the crumbs were collected, absorbed and demolished as by an immense vacuum cleaner, and yielded to an uncontrollable mass of dark that came tumbling in through windows and doors to take their place. Darkness infested the building like a flight of bats returning willingly to roost.

"Wash hands, please. Wash hands, please," the intercom began to bawl in the passage at four-forty-five. Without much need of prompting the staff hustled like lemmings along the corridors to the green and blue-tiled washrooms that mocked the encroaching dusk with an illusion of cheerfulness.

"All papers into cases, please," the Tannoy* warned, five minutes later. "Look at your desks, ladies and gentlemen. Any documents left lying about? Kindly put them away. Desks must be left clear and tidy. Drawers must be shut."

A multitudinous shuffling, a rustling as of innumerable bluebottles might have been heard by the attentive ear after this injunction, as the employees of Moreton Wold and Company thrust their papers into briefcases, clipped statistical abstracts together and slammed them into filing cabinets; dropped discarded copy into wastepaper baskets. Two minutes later, and not a desk throughout Grimes Buildings bore more than its customary coating of dust.

"Hats and coats on, please. Hats and coats on, please. Did you bring an umbrella? Have you left any shopping on the floor?"

At three minutes to five the home-going throng was in the lifts and on the stairs; a clattering staccato-voiced flood momentarily darkened the great double doors of the building, and then as the first faint notes of St. Paul's* came echoing faintly on the frosty air, to be picked up near at hand by the louder chime of St. Biddulph's on the Wall*, the entire premises of Moreton Wold stood empty.

"But why is it?" Jason Ashgrove, the new copywriter, asked his secretary. "Why are the staff herded out so fast in the evenings? Not that I'm against it, mind you, I think it's an admirable idea in many ways, but there is the liberty of the individual to be considered, don't you think?"

"Hush!" Miss Golden, casting a glance towards the door, held up her felt-tip in warning or reproof. "You mustn't ask that sort of question. When you are taken on to the Established Staff you'll be told. Not before."

"But I want to know now," said Jason in discontent. "Do you know?"

"Yes I do," Miss Golden answered tantalizingly. "Come on, or we shan't have done the Oat Crisp layout by a quarter to." And she stared firmly down at the copy in front of her, lips folded, candy-floss hair falling over her face, lashes hiding eyes like peridots*, a girl with a secret.

Jason was annoyed. He rapped out a couple of rude and witty rhymes which Miss Golden let pass in a withering silence.

"What do you want for Christmas, Miss Golden? Sherry? Fudge? Bath cubes?"

"I want to go away with a clear conscience about Oat Crisps," Miss Golden retorted. It was not true; what she chiefly wanted was Mr. Jason Ashgrove, but he had not realized this yet.

"Come on, don't be a tease! I'm sure you haven't been on the Established Staff all that long," he coaxed her. "What happens when one is taken on, anyway? Does the Managing Director have us up for a confidential chat? Or are we given a little book called The Awful Secret of Grimes Buildings?"

Miss Golden wasn't telling. She opened her desk drawer and took out a white towel and a cake of rosy soap.

"Wash hands, please! Wash hands, please!"

Jason was frustrated. "You'll be sorry," he said. "I shall do something desperate."

"Oh no, you mustn't!" Her eyes were large with fright. She ran from the room and was back within a couple of minutes, still drying her hands.

"If I took you out to dinner, wouldn't you give me just a tiny hint?"

Side by side Miss Golden and Mr. Ashgrove ran along the green-floored corridors, battled down the white marble stairs, among the hundred other employees from the tenth floor, and the nine hundred from the floors below.

He saw her lips move as she said something, but in the clatter of two thousand feet the words were lost.

"...f-f-fire escape," he heard, as they came into the momentary hush of the coir-carpeted* entrance hall. And "...it's to do with a bicycle. A bicycle and a harp."

"I don't understand."

Now they were in the street, chilly with the winter-dusk smells of celery on barrows, of swept-up leaves heaped in far-away parks, and cold layers of dew sinking among the withered evening primroses in the building sites. London lay about them wreathed in twilit mystery and fading against the barred and smoky sky. Like a ninth wave the sound of traffic overtook and swallowed them.

"Please tell me!"

But, shaking her head, she stepped on to a scarlet homebound bus and was borne away from him.

Jason stood undecided on the pavement, with the crowds dividing round him as round the pier of a bridge. He scratched his head and looked about him for guidance.

An ambulance clanged, a taxi screeched, a drill stuttered,

a siren wailed on the river, a door slammed, a van hooted, and close beside his ear a bicycle bell tinkled its tiny warning.

A bicycle, she had said. A bicycle and a harp.

Jason turned and stared at Grimes Buildings.

Somewhere, he knew, there was a back way in, a service entrance. He walked slowly past the main doors, with their tubs of snowy chrysanthemums, and on up Glass Street. A tiny furtive wedge of darkness beckoned him, a snicket, a hacket, an alley carved into the thickness of the building. It was so narrow that at any moment, it seemed, the over-topping walls would come together and squeeze it out of existence.

Walking as softly as an Indian, Jason passed through it, slid by a file of dustbins, and found the foot of the fire escape. Iron treads rose into the mist, like an illustration to a Gothic fairytale.

He began to climb.

When he had mounted to the ninth storey he paused for breath. It was a lonely place. The lighting consisted of a dim bulb at the foot of every flight. A well of gloom sank beneath him. The cold fingers of the wind nagged and fluttered at the edges of his jacket, and he pulled the string of the fire door and edged inside.

Grimes Buildings were triangular, with the street forming the base of the triangle, and the fire escape the point. Jason could see two long passages coming towards him, meeting at an acute angle where he stood. He started down the left-hand one, tiptoeing in the cave-like silence. Nowhere was there any sound, except for the faraway drip of a tap. No night watchman would stay in the building; none was needed. No precautions were taken. Burglars gave the place a wide berth.

Jason opened a door at random; then another. Offices lay everywhere about him, empty and forbidding. Some held lipstick-stained tissues, spilt powder, and orange peel; others were still foggy with cigarette smoke. Here was a director's suite of rooms—a desk like half an acre of frozen lake, inch-thick carpet, roses, and the smell of cigars. Here was a conference room with scattered squares of doodled blotting paper. All equally empty.

He was not sure when he first began to notice the bell. Telephone, he thought at first, and then he remembered that all the outside lines were disconnected at five. And this bell, anyway, had not the regularity of a telephone's double ring: there was a tinkle, and then silence: a long ring, and then silence: a whole volley of rings together, and then silence.

Jason stood listening, and fear knocked against his ribs and shortened his breath. He knew that he must move or be paralysed by it. He ran up a flight of stairs and found himself with two more endless green corridors beckoning him like a pair of dividers.

Another sound now: a waft of ice-thin notes, riffling up an arpeggio like a flurry of sleet. Far away down the passage it echoed. Jason ran in pursuit, but as he ran the music receded. He circled the building, but it always outdistanced him, and when he came back to the stairs, he heard it fading away on to the storey below.

He hesitated, and as he did so, heard once more the bell: the bicycle bell. It was approaching him fast, bearing down on him, urgent, menacing. He could hear the pedals, almost see the shimmer of an invisible wheel. Absurdly, he was reminded of the insistent clamour of an ice-cream vendor, summoning children on a sultry Sunday afternoon.

There was a little fireman's alcove beside him, with buckets and pumps. He hurled himself into it. The bell stopped beside him, and then there was a moment while his heart tried to shake itself loose in his chest. He was looking into two eyes carved out of expressionless air; he was held by two hands knotted together out of the width of dark.

"Daisy? Daisy?" came the whisper. "Is that you, Daisy? Have you come to give me your answer?"

Jason tried to speak, but no words came.

"It's *not* Daisy! Who are you?" The sibilants were full of threat. "You can't stay here! This is private property."

He was thrust along the corridor. It was like being pushed by a whirlwind—the fire door opened ahead of him without a touch, and he was on the openwork platform, clutching the slender rail. Still the hands would not let him go.

"How about it?" the whisper mocked him. "How about jumping? It's an easy death compared with some."

Jason looked down into the smoky void. The darkness nodded to him like a familiar.*

"You wouldn't be much loss, would you?" What have you got to live for?"

Miss Golden, Jason thought. She would miss me. And the syllables Berenice Golden lingered in the air like a chime. Drawing on some unknown deposit of courage he shook himself loose from the holding hands, and ran down the fire escape without looking back.

Next morning when Miss Golden, crisp, fragrant and punctual, shut the door of Room 92 behind her, she stopped short by the hat-pegs with a horrified gasp.

"Mr. *Ashgrove*! Your *hair*!"

"It makes me look very distinguished, don't you think?" he said.

It did indeed have this effect, for his Byronic* dark cut had changed to a stippled silver.

"How did it happen? You've not—" her voice sank to a whisper—"*You've not been in Grimes Buildings after dark?*"

"What if I have?"

"Have you?"

"Miss Golden—Berenice," he said earnestly. "Who was Daisy? I can see that you know. Tell me her story."

"Did you see him?" she asked faintly.

"Him?"

"William Heron—the Wailing Watchman. Oh," she exclaimed in terror. "I can see that you must have. Then you are doomed—doomed!"

"If I'm doomed," said Jason, "let's have coffee and you tell me all about it."

"It all happened over fifty years ago," said Berenice, as she spooned out coffee powder with distracted extravagance. "Heron was the night watchman in this building, patrolling the corridors from dusk to dawn every night on his bicycle. He fell in love with a Miss Bell who taught the harp. She rented a room—this room—and gave lessons in it. She began to reciprocate his love, and they used to share a picnic supper every night at eleven, and she'd stay on a while to keep him company. It was an idyll, among the fire buckets and the furnace pipes.

"On Christmas Eve he had summoned up the courage to propose to her. The day before he had told her that he was going to ask her a very important question. Next night he came to the Buildings with a huge bunch of roses and a bottle of wine. But Miss Bell never turned up.

"The explanation was simple. Miss Bell, of course, had been losing a lot of sleep through her nocturnal romance, as she gave lessons all day, and so she used to take a nap in her music room between seven and ten every evening, to save going home. In order to make sure that she would wake up, she persuaded her father, a distant relation of Graham Bell who shared some of the more famous Bell's mechanical ingenuity, to install an alarm device, a kind of telephone, in her room, which called her every evening at ten. She was far too modest and shy to let Heron know that she spent those hours actually in the building, and to give him the chance of waking her himself.

"Alas! On this important evening the gadget failed and she never woke up. Telephones were in their infancy at that time, you must remember.

"Heron waited and waited. At last, mad with grief and jealousy, having rung up her home and discovered that she was not there, he concluded that she had rejected him, ran to the fire escape, and cast himself off it, holding the roses and the bottle of wine. He jumped from the tenth floor.

"Daisy did not long survive him, but pined away soon after; since that day their ghosts have haunted Grimes Buildings, he vainly patrolling the corridors on his bicycle in search of her, she playing her harp in the small room she rented. *But they never meet.* And anyone who meets the ghost of William Heron will himself within five days leap down from the same fatal fire escape."

She gazed at him with tragic eyes.

"In that case we mustn't lose a minute," said Jason and he enveloped her in an embrace as prolonged as it was ardent. Looking down at the gossamer hair sprayed across his shoulder, he added, "Just the same, it is a preposterous situation. Firstly, I have no intention of jumping off the fire escape—" here, however, he repressed a shudder as he remembered the cold, clutching hands of the evening before—"And secondly, I find it quite nonsensical that those two inefficient ghosts have spent fifty years in this building without coming across each other. We must remedy the matter, Berenice. We must not begrudge our new-found happiness to others."

He gave her another kiss so impassioned that the electric typewriter against which they were leaning began chattering to itself in a frenzy of enthusiasm.

"This very evening," he went on, looking at his watch, "we will put matters right for that unhappy couple, and then, if I really have only five more days to live, which I don't for one moment believe, we will proceed to spend them together, my bewitching Berenice, in the most advantageous manner possible."

She nodded, spellbound.

"Can you work a switchboard?" She nodded again. "My love, you are perfection itself. Meet me in the switchboard room, then, at ten this evening. I would say, have dinner with me, but I shall need to make one or two purchases and see an old RAF* friend. You will be safe from Heron's curse in the switchboard room if he always keeps to the corridors."

"I would rather meet him and die with you," she murmured.

"My angel, I hope that won't be necessary. Now," he said sighing, "I suppose we should get down to our day's work." Strangely enough, the copy they wrote that day, although engendered from such agitated minds, sold more packets of Oat Crisps than any other advertising matter before or since.

That evening when Jason entered Grimes Buildings he was carrying two bottles of wine, two bunches of red roses, and a large canvas-covered bundle. Miss Golden, who had concealed herself in the telephone exchange before the offices closed for the night, gazed at these things with interest.

"Now," said Jason after he had greeted her, "I want you first of all to ring our own extension."

"No one will reply, surely?"

"I think *she* will reply."

Sure enough, when Berenice rang extension 170 a faint, sleepy voice, distant and yet clear, whispered, "Hullo?"

"Is that Miss Bell?"

"...Yes."

Berenice went a little pale. Her eyes sought Jason's and, prompted by him, she said formally, "Switchboard here, Miss Bell, your ten o'clock call."

"Thank you," whispered the telephone.

"Excellent," Jason remarked, as Miss Golden replaced the receiver with a trembling hand. He unfastened his package and slipped its straps over his shoulder. "Now, plug in the intercom."

Berenice did so, and then announced, loudly and clearly, "Attention. Night watchman on duty, please. Night watchman on duty. You have an urgent summons to Room 92. You have an urgent summons to Room 92."

Her voice echoed and reverberated through the empty corridors, then the Tannoy coughed itself to silence.

"Now we must run. You take the roses, sweetheart, and I'll carry the bottles."

Together they raced up eight flights of stairs and along the green corridor to Room 92. As they neared the door a burst of music met them—harp music swelling out, sweet and triumphant. Jason took one of the bunches of roses from Berenice, opened the door a little way, and gently deposited the flowers, with the bottle, inside the door. As he closed it again Berenice said breathlessly, "Did you see anything?"

"No," he said. "The room was too full of music."

His eyes were shining.

They stood hand in hand, reluctant to move away, waiting for they hardly knew what. Suddenly the door flew open again. Neither Berenice nor Jason, afterwards, cared to speak of what they saw then, but each was left with a memory, bright as the picture on a Salvador Dali* calendar, of a bicycle bearing on its saddle a harp, a bottle of wine, and a bouquet of red roses, sweeping improbably down the corridor and far, far away.

"We can go now," said Jason. He led Berenice to the fire door, tucking the other bottle of Mâcon* into his jacket pocket. A black wind from the north whistled beneath, as they stood on the openwork iron platform, looking down.

"We don't want our evening to be spoilt by the thought of that curse hanging over us," he said, "so this is the practical thing to do. Hang on to the roses." And holding his love firmly, Jason pulled the ripcord of his RAF friend's parachute and leapt off the fire escape.

A bridal shower of rose petals adorned the descent of Miss Golden, who was possibly the only girl to be kissed in mid-air in the district of Clerkenwell at ten minutes to midnight on Christmas Eve.

* **Tannoy:** intercom system

* **St. Paul's, St. Biddulph's on the Wall :** large, domed cathedrals in London, England, with chimes to mark the time

* **peridot:** olive-green chrysolite or gem

* **coir-carpeted:** coir—a coconut fibre used to make ropes and mats.

* **familiar:** animal or spirit attending on and obeying a witch

* **Byronic:** reference to the 19th-century English poet, Lord Byron, whose dark good looks made him something of a cult figure. Here, it refers to Jason's longish hair style.

* **RAF:** Royal Air Force (British)

* **Salvador Dali:** 20th-century Spanish artist best known for his surrealist landscape paintings

* **Mâcon:** a red wine made in France

The Soft Voice of
The Serpent

NADINE GORDIMER

He was only twenty-six and very healthy and he was soon strong enough to be wheeled out into the garden. Like everyone else, he had great and curious faith in the garden: "Well, soon you'll be up and able to sit out in the garden," they said, looking at him fervently, with little understanding tilts of the head. Yes, he would be out...in the garden. It was a big garden enclosed in old dark, sleek, pungent firs, and he could sit deep beneath their tiered fringes, down in the shade, far away. There was the feeling that there, in the garden, he would come to an understanding; that it would come easier, there. Perhaps there was something in this of the old Eden idea; the tender human adjusting himself to himself in the soothing impersonal presence of trees and grass and earth, before going out into the stare of the world.

The very first time it was so strange; his wife was wheeling him along the gravel path in the sun and the shade, and he felt exactly as he did when he was a little boy and he used to bend and hang, looking at the world upside down, through his ankles. Everything was vast and open, the sky, the wind blowing along through the swaying, trembling greens, the flowers shaking in vehement denial. Movement....

A first slight wind lifted again in the slack, furled sail of himself; he felt it belly gently, so gently he could just feel it, lifting inside him.

So she wheeled him along, pushing hard and not particularly well with her thin pretty arms—but he would not for anything complain of the way she did it or suggest that the nurse might do better, for he knew that would hurt her—and when they came to a spot that he liked, she put the brake on the chair and settled him there for the morning. That was the first time and now he sat there every day. He read a lot, but his attention was arrested sometimes, quite suddenly and compellingly, by the sunken place under the rug where his leg used to be. There was his one leg, and next to it, the rug flapped loose. Then looking, he felt his leg not there; he felt it go, slowly, from the toe to the thigh. He felt that he had no leg. After a few minutes he went back to his book. He never let the realization quite reach him; he let himself realize it physically, but he never quite let it get at *him*. He felt it pressing up, coming, coming, dark, crushing, ready to burst—but he always turned away, just in time, back to his book. That was his system; that was the way he was going to do it. He would let it come near, irresistibly near, again and again, ready to catch him alone in the garden. And again and again he would turn it back, just in time. Slowly it would become a habit, with the reassuring strength of a habit. It would become such a habit never to get to the point of realizing it, *that he never would realize it*. And one day he would find that he had achieved what he wanted: *he would feel as if he had always been like that*.

Then the danger would be over, forever.

In a week or two he did not have to read all the time; he could let himself put down the book and look about him, watching the firs part silkily as a child's fine straight hair in the wind, watching the small birds tightroping the telephone wire, watching the fat old dove trotting after his refined patrician gray women, purring with lust. His wife came and sat beside him, doing her sewing, and sometimes they spoke, but often they sat for hours, a whole morning, her movements at work small and unobtrusive as the birds', he resting his head back and looking at a blur of sky through half-closed eyes. Now and then her eye, habitually looking inwards, would catch the signal of some little happening, some point of color in the garden, and her laugh or exclamation drawing his attention to it would suddenly clear away the silence.

At eleven o'clock she would get up and put down her sewing and go into the house to fetch their tea; crunching slowly away into the sun up the path, going easily, empowered by the sun rather than her own muscles. He watched her go, easily.... He was healing. In the static quality of his gaze, in the relaxed feeling of his mouth, in the upward-lying palm of his hand, there was annealment....

One day a big locust whirred dryly past her head, and she jumped up with a cry, scattering her sewing things. He laughed at her as she bent about picking them up, shuddering. She went into the house to fetch the tea, and he began to read. But presently he put down the book and, yawning, noticed a reel of pink cotton that she had missed, lying in a rose bed.

He smiled, remembering her. And then he became conscious of a curious old-mannish little face, fixed upon him in a kind of hypnotic dread. There, absolutely stilled with fear beneath his glance, crouched a very big locust. What an amusing face the thing had! A lugubrious long face, that somehow suggested a bald head, and such a glum mouth. It looked like some little person out of a Disney cartoon. It moved slightly, still looking up fearfully at him. Strange body, encased in a sort of old-fashioned creaky armor. He had never realized before what ridiculous-looking insects locusts were! Well, naturally not; they occur to one collectively, as a pest—one doesn't go around looking at their faces.

The face was certainly curiously human and even expressive, but looking at the body, he decided that the body couldn't really be called a body at all. With the face, the creature's kinship with humans ended. The body was flimsy paper stretched over a frame of matchstick, like a small boy's homemade airplane. And those could not be thought of as legs—the great saw-toothed back ones were like the parts of an old crane, and the front ones like—like one of her hairpins, bent in two. At that moment the creature slowly lifted up one of the front legs, and passed it tremblingly over its head, stroking the left antenna down. Just as a man might take out a handkerchief and pass it over his brow.

He began to feel enormously interested in the creature, and leaned over in his chair to see it more closely. It sensed him and beneath its stiff, plated sides, he was surprised to see the pulsations of a heart. How fast it was breathing.... He leaned away a little, to frighten it less.

Watching it carefully, and trying to keep himself effaced from its consciousness by not moving, he became aware of some struggle going on in the thing. It seemed to gather itself together in muscular concentration: this co-ordinated force then passed along its body in a kind of petering tremor, and ended in a stirring along the upward shaft of the great back legs. But the locust remained where it was. Several times this wave of effort currented through it and was spent, but the next time it ended surprisingly in a few hobbling, uneven steps, undercarriage—airplanelike again—trailing along the earth.

Then the creature lay, fallen on its side, antennae turned stretched out toward him. It groped with its hands, feeling for a hold on the soft ground, bending its elbows and straining. With a heave, it righted itself, and as it did so, he saw—leaning forward again—what was the trouble. It was the same trouble. His own trouble. The creature had lost one leg. Only the long upward shaft of its left leg remained, with a neat round aperture where, no doubt, the other half of the leg had been jointed in.

Now as he watched the locust gather itself again and again in that concentration of muscle, spend itself again and again in a message that was so puzzlingly never obeyed, he knew exactly what the creature felt. Of course he knew that feeling! That absolute certainty that the leg was there: one had only to lift it.... The upward shaft of the locust's leg quivered, lifted; why then couldn't he walk? He tried again. The message came; it was going through, the leg was lifting, now it was ready—now!... The shaft sagged in the air, with nothing, nothing to hold it up.

He laughed and shook his head: He *knew*...Good Lord, *exactly* like—He called out to the house—"Come quickly! Come and see! You've got another patient!"

"What?" she shouted. "I'm getting tea."

"Come and look!" he called. "Now!"

"...What is it?" she said, approaching the locust distastefully.

"Your locust!" he said. She jumped away with a little shriek.

"Don't worry—it can't move. It's as harmless as I am. You must have knocked its leg off when you hit out at it!" He was laughing at her.

"Oh, I didn't!" she said reproachfully. She loathed it but she loathed to hurt, even more. "I never even touched it! All I hit was air...I couldn't possibly have hit it. Not its leg off."

"All right then. It's another locust. But it's lost its leg, anyway. You should just see it.... It doesn't know the leg isn't there. God, I know exactly how that feels.... I've been watching it, and honestly, it's uncanny. I can see it feels just like I do!"

She smiled at him, sideways; she seemed suddenly pleased at something. Then, recalling herself, she came forward, bent double, hands upon her hips.

"Well, if it can't move...," she said, hanging over it.

"Don't be frightened," he laughed. "Touch it."

"Ah, the poor thing," she said, catching her breath in compassion. "It can't walk."

"Don't encourage it to self-pity," he teased her.

She looked up and laughed. "Oh you—" she parried, assuming a frown. The locust kept its solemn silly face turned to her. "Shame, isn't he a funny old man," she said, "But what will happen to him?"

"I don't know," he said, for being in the same boat absolved him from responsibility or pity. "Maybe he'll grow another one. Lizards grow new tails, if they lose them."

"Oh, *lizards*," she said. "—But not these. I'm afraid the cat'll get him."

"Get another little chair made for him and you can wheel him out here with me."

"Yes," she laughed. "Only for him it would have to be a kind of little cart, with wheels."

"Or maybe he could be taught to use crutches. I'm sure the farmers would like to know that he was being kept active."

"The poor old thing," she said, bending over the locust again. And reaching back somewhere into an inquisitive childhood she picked up a thin wand of twig and prodded the locust, very gently. "Funny thing is, it's even the same leg, the left one." She looked round at him and smiled.

"I know," he nodded, laughing. "The two of us..." And then he shook his head and, smiling, said it again: "The two of us."

She was laughing and just then she flicked the twig more sharply than she meant to and at the touch of it there was a sudden flurried papery whirr, and the locust flew away.

She stood there with the stick in her hand, half afraid of it again, and appealed, unnerved as a child, "What happened. What happened."

There was a moment of silence.

"Don't be a fool," he said irritably.

They had forgotten that locusts can fly.

Making Poison

MARGARET ATWOOD

When I was five my brother and I made poison. We were living in a city then, but we probably would have made the poison anyway. We kept it in a paint can under somebody else's house and we put all the poisonous things into it that we could think of: toadstools, dead mice, mountain ash berries which may not have been poisonous but looked it, piss which we saved up in order to add it to the paint can. By the time the can was full everything in it was very poisonous.

The problem was that once having made the poison we couldn't just leave it there. We had to do something with it. We didn't want to put it into anyone's food, but we wanted an object, a completion. There was no one we hated enough, that was the difficulty.

I can't remember what we did with the poison in the end. Did we leave it under the corner of the house, which was made of wood and brownish yellow? Did we throw it at someone, some innocuous child? We wouldn't have dared an adult. Is this a true image I have, a small face streaming with tears and red berries, the sudden knowledge that the poison was really poisonous after all? Or did we throw it out, do I remember those red berries floating down a gutter, into a culvert, am I innocent?

Why did we make the poison in the first place? I can remember the glee with which we stirred and added, the sense of magic and accomplishment. Making poison is as much fun as making a cake. People like to make poison. If you don't understand this you will never understand anything.

The Three Thieves

GEOFFREY CHAUCER

In Flanders some years ago there were three young men who lived a life of folly and wickedness. They spent their time drinking and gambling in taverns, playing dice night and day, throwing away money on dancing girls, and eating and drinking far more than they either needed or could possibly use. Their curses were so foul and blood-curdling that it was really terrifying to hear them swear. Each of them laughed greatly at the others' sins. Needless to say, they could not get enough money by honest means to live such a life.

One day these three young men were sitting in a tavern drinking, although it was still quite early in the morning. While they were sitting there, they heard a bell tolling as a funeral procession passed by. One of them called to the serving boy and said, "Go out at once, and find out what corpse this is that is passing by—and make sure that you report his name correctly."

"Sir," said the boy, "there is no need to ask. I heard all about it before you came here, two hours ago. He was an old companion of yours. Last night he was here in the tavern, sitting in his usual place, and very, very drunk, and suddenly he was slain. There came a thief called Death, who slays all the people in this land. He struck your friend in the heart with his spear—and went on his way. He has slain at least a thousand during this plague. Master, in case you meet him yourself, you had better beware of him. This is what my mother taught me; I don't know any more about it."

"By Saint Mary," said the tavern keeper, "the boy is right. This year Death has slain so many men, women, and children in a little village about a mile from here that I expect he must live there! Certainly it is best to be very careful and always be on the watch to avoid him."

"By heaven," said one of the drunken men, "is it then so dangerous to meet him? For myself, I vow I shall seek him in every highway and byway. Listen, comrades, we three should be in this together. Let each of us hold up his hand and swear to be a brother to the others, and help them in all things, and then we will slay this false traitor Death. He, that slays so many others, shall himself be slain before nightfall!"

The others agreed, and all three swore to live and die together as brothers. Up they jumped in their drunken rage and started towards the village which the tavern keeper had mentioned. By many a grim and bloody oath they vowed that Death would die if they could catch him.

When they had gone not quite half a mile, they met a wretched-looking old man. He greeted them politely and meekly, and said, "God protect you, my lords."

The proudest of the three answered with a sneer, "Well, fellow, you're certainly a sorry sight! Why are you all wrapped up, except for your face? Why do you go on living so long, as old as you are?"

The old man looked him full in the face, and said quietly, "Why? Because I could not find a man anywhere, even if I walked from here to India, who would exchange his youth for my old age. Therefore I must keep my age as long as it is God's will. Nor will Death take my life. So I must walk like a restless captive. On the ground, which is my mother's gate, I knock with my staff and say, `Dear mother, let me in! Look how I am fading away, flesh, and blood, and breath. Alas, when shall my bones be at rest?' But still she will not grant my wish, and that is why my face is pale and withered.

"But, sirs, it is not courteous of you to speak so rudely to an old man. Let me give you some advice: Do not harm an old man now any more than you wish men to harm you when you are old—if you live to be the same age. Now God be with you, wherever you go; I must be on my way."

"Oh no you don't, you old rogue," said another of the three. "By Saint John, you're not getting away from us that easily. You spoke just now of that traitor Death, who kills all our friends in this country. Since you seem to be his spy, tell us where he is, or we'll make you pay dearly for it! False thief, we know you're on his side, planning to slay us young folk!"

"Sirs," said the old man, "if you are so eager to find Death, turn up this crooked path. I left him there in the wood, under a tree, and there he shall stay. I assure you your boasts won't make him hide. Do you see that oak? You'll find him right there. May God save you, and may He help you to mend your ways."

None of them paid any further attention to the old man, for at once they all ran to the tree he had pointed out. But there, to their enormous delight and astonishment, they saw a huge pile of shining gold coins—there seemed to be about eight bushels of them. They forgot all about looking for Death, since each of them was overjoyed at the dazzling sight of the bright gold. They sat down to gaze at this precious pile, and the worst of the three was the first to speak. "Brothers," said he, "pay careful attention to what I say. My wits are sharp, even if I usually seem to use them only in joke. Fortune has given us this treasure so that we can live our lives in jollity and games. It came lightly, and it is right that we should spend it lightly. Who would have thought that we should have such luck today? But the gold must be carried home from this place to my house—or yours—before we can really enjoy it. However, we certainly can't do it by day, for then people would say that we were bold thieves and hang us for taking our own treasure. It must be carried away by night, as slyly and secretly as possible. So I suggest that we draw lots, and he whose lot it is shall immediately run to the town and bring us all bread and wine. The other two will keep guard over the treasure while he is gone. Then when it is night, we'll take the treasure to whatever place we all agree is best. Here, brothers—draw lots."

They drew lots, and the lot fell to the youngest. He started out towards the town at once. As soon as he had gone, the one who had suggested the plan turned to the other, and said, "You know that you are my sworn brother. Now I'm going to tell you something for your own good. You know well that our comrade is gone, and here we have a great deal of gold which is to be divided among the three of us. However, if I can manage things so that it will only be divided among the two of us, won't I be doing a favor for you?"

The other answered, "I don't know how that can be done. He knows that we have the gold. What shall we do? What can we say to him?"

"If you'll swear to secrecy," said the first villain, "I'll tell you in a few words what we can do."

"I swear it," said the other. "I wouldn't dream of betraying you."

"Now then," said the first, "you know well that we are two, and two of us are bound to be stronger than one. As soon as he comes back and sits down, you get up as if you wanted to wrestle with him in fun. While you struggle with him, as if in play, I'll stab him in the side and back. At the same time, you draw your own dagger and do likewise. Then, dear friend, all this gold shall be divided between you and me. We two can have everything we desire, and play at dice to our heart's content."

And so the two villains agreed between themselves to slay the third in this manner. Meanwhile, the youngest of the three, as he went to the town, thought a good deal about the beauty of the bright gold coins. "Lord," he said to himself, "if only I could have all this treasure to myself alone, there wouldn't be a man in the world who could live more merrily than I." And it wasn't long before it came into his mind that he could buy poison, in order to kill both his companions and get all the gold for himself.

Walking at a fast pace, he wasted no time. He went at once to a druggist in the town and asked him for some poison to kill the rats in his barn, as well as a skunk which, he said, was carrying off all his chickens. The druggist was sympathetic, and assured him, "I'll give you something that no creature alive can eat or drink without losing his life. Even if he has a bit of it as small as a grain of wheat, this poison is so strong and deadly, he shall die in less time than it takes to walk a mile."

The villain was well pleased with this recommendation and bought the poison. He took the box in his hand and went on to a shop in the next street. There he bought three bottles of wine, and in two of them he poured his poison. The third he kept pure for himself, knowing he would need it to give him the strength to work all night carrying away all the gold.

When he returned to his comrades they killed him in the manner that they had planned. When that was done, one of them said, "Now let's sit and drink and be merry; we'll bury his body later." And as he spoke he happened to pick up one of the poisoned bottles, and drank from it, and gave his comrade a drink from it also. And so they were both poisoned.

Thus were the two murderers slain, and the false poisoner as well. They had found Death under the oak tree, although they had not recognized him in the pile of gold.

An Afternoon in Bright Sunlight

S. BRUISED HEAD

A YISSOMAAWA*...

The Porcupine Hills look soft and brown as we stand gazing out over sunburnt prairie grass.

"Come on, guys. Let's go for a ride," says Hank.

Hank is boss. At least he thinks he is. He is a year older than Anne and me and is the only boy in the family. We let him get away with it, sometimes.

Anne agrees with him. She always agrees with him, especially when we have nothing to do. "We'll ask mom to make some sandwiches."

"Good idea. Tell her we're going to hunt arrowheads."

Hank decides Anne will ride Brownie, a twelve-year-old bay gelding, same age as Hank. He chooses Hoss for me. Hank says, "Hoss needs some kinks worked out, and this is as good a day as any." He chooses Buck, because Buck is his horse and Buck understands him.

Mom packs enough food to last a week, and, as we make our way back to the corral, she comes to the door and yells, "Don't go too far into the coulee*, and watch out for rattlesnakes." She mangles a dish-towel. "Keep an eye open for that bear Jerry saw last week. He says he spotted it down by the old school and later saw it moving toward the hills." She shakes out the towel and waves it. "Get home before dark." She smiles. "Have a good time."

"All right," I yell. "We'll be careful."

"Don't let her worry you." Anne picks up the sack. "There are no rattlesnakes in the coulee, and you know Jerry lies a lot."

"I know Jerry lies. I'm not worried."

Hank has the horses saddled and ready to go. He takes the sack and ties it to the back of his saddle.

A wide streak of dust rises, billows out, and kind of hangs in the air. "There's Dad," says Hank. He pats Buck's neck.

Mom doesn't look too pleased. The dust mushrooms. We hear Dad's loud laughing voice, "Hello Dawlink!" Mom takes a swipe at him with her dish-towel. "I brought company," he says.

"Isn't that old Sam?" says Hank.

Mom shakes hands with Sam; her voice carries on the breeze. "Come in. I'll make you something to eat."

Everybody treats Sam with respect. I remember walking in front of him one time, and, boy, did I ever get it from Dad. I stay out of his way, now.

Hank is all excited. "There's Les!"

Les comes running. We all think Les is the greatest. Dad picks him up whenever he needs help. He trains horses for Dad. He trained Hoss, and helps out during calving season. He travels with Dad, and, sometimes, he even drives. He seems older than fourteen.

"Hey, Les," says Hank. "You can ride Hoss."

"Where you going?" Les lengthens the stirrups.

"Hunting arrowheads."

Anne and I stand there listening. They ignore us. They always ignore us.

"Hey! You kids!" shouts Dad from the house. Hank shoves me and Anne up on Brownie, and we take off. We can hear Dad shouting. We reach the coulee, and Hank reins in. Les looks at him.

"Your Dad was calling."

"I know."

"You guys are in trouble."

"He wants us to stay home."

"Well," says Les. "We might as well keep going now. We'll catch heck for one thing or another."

"I know, but maybe if we stay out late, he'll cool off."

"Yeah, he'll get worried," says Anne.

"Yeah, he'll just have more to get mad about," I say.

They just look at me.

We wander into the coulees, stopping every now and then to pick cactus berries. They are green and plump, the size of grapes. Their juice is sweet and sticky. They are easy to find in the short grass, and we go from patch to patch.

As we near an outcropping of rock, Anne says, "Mom said to watch out for rattlesnakes."

"Don't be silly. Everybody knows there are no rattlesnakes in these coulees. Right, Hank?"

Hank and I agree.

"Well, how about that bear Jerry saw?" says Anne.

"Jerry didn't see no bear," laughs Les.

"Are you sure?" Hank licks his lips whenever he's worried. He does it now.

"Sure I'm sure. There hasn't been a bear in these coulees for years."

"Well, a bear could have come down from the hills."

"Look," says Les, "there are no bears in this coulee."

That settles the bear question. We stay away from the rocks. Everybody knows that snakes sun themselves on rocks. None of us likes snakes, especially Hank and Anne.

Hank licks his lips. "Jerry lies a lot."

"You still worried?" says Les.

"I just remembered Dad said he saw something out here."

"I remember, too," says Anne eagerly. "It was the day before Jerry came to visit."

"It was after," I say.

"It was before," says Hank.

Anne smiles at me. "I told you," she says.

"Come to think of it," says Les, "just before we came out, we were at the pool hall in town. Your dad, Sam, and some other men were talking about seeing something out here."

"What did they see?"

"Do you know anything about Sam?"

"Yeah. He's old, and he lives by the school," says Hank.

"You're not supposed to walk in front of him," I say. "Did you know that?"

Anne wants to know more. "What about him?"

Les looks at Hank. "Do you know why he lives there?"

"No."

"He guards the coulees."

We look at Les. He looks back. He isn't smiling. His eyes sweep over us. Then he turns and carefully guides Hoss around a clump of brittle reeds down onto a dry creek bed.

"What do you mean, he guards the coulees?"

"Just that."

"Why should he guard the coulees?" Les has me curious, too.

"Oh," says Les. "There's things out here."

"What kind of things?"

"Animals...other things that live in the coulee."

"You've got to be kidding. Only animals live in the coulee." Hank shakes his head and laughs.

"What kind of things?" I insist.

"You don't have to know," Hank cuts in. "What did old Sam have to say?"

In a matter-of-fact tone, Les says, "He thinks a wolverine* may have moved in."

"A wolverine? No kidding!" Hank's eyes light up. He moves closer to Les. "Maybe we should forget about arrowheads and go hunting."

"I don't think so."

"But, I've never seen a wolverine. It would be fun."

"We better wait until Sam figures out what to do."

"What does Sam have to do with anything?"

"Sam knows a lot. He says they're dangerous."

I break in. "That's what Emma said."

"Yeah? What did Emma have to say?"

"You're not supposed to listen to Emma," says Anne.

"Well, she says they're dangerous and evil, too."

"Forget about Emma," Hank says, licking his lips. "She's a crazy old lady. Just how dangerous are wolverines?"

"Well, you know that bear?" says Les.

"Yeah?"

"Well, wolverines hunt the hunter."

Hank looks over his shoulder. Anne and I smile.

It is hot. Horse tails switch lazily at slow-moving flies. Saddle leather squeaks. Hooves thud dully on dry grass. An occasional sharp crack echoes down the coulee.

She stands listening to the children's voices. An outcropping of rock hides her den. Inside, it is cool and dry.

Ayisomaawaawa...I must be careful, I waited long. Need to grow. Strong. Strong. Strong as when I was young. It was good. Our power was strong. Must be careful. Haste betrays. I must wait. Come, boy. Come alone. Do not fear. There is nothing to fear.

"Hank!" Anne yells. "Look at the chokecherries!"

Low chokecherry bushes grow halfway up the side of the coulee. Their branches hang with thick clusters of black cherries.

"Let's pick some for mom," I say.

Hank dismounts. "Good idea, Girlie. Here, you hold the horses."

"Why do I always have to hold the horses?"

"Because I tell you to."

I look down at him. "We can't pick berries, anyway."

"Why not?"

"We have nothing to put them in."

"We can put them in the lunch sack," says Anne.

"Good idea," says Hank. "We can tie the horses up down by those bushes."

I must wait. Cannot hurry. Wait. Not strong. Stronger must wait. Soon. Soon. So close.

The bushes are low and evenly spaced. They look as if they were planted by someone. Anne and I fill our hats and empty the berries into the sack. We begin filling our hats again, when Anne spots some raspberries growing near the outcropping of rock.

"Come on, Hank. Let's get some of them, too."

"I'm not going over there."

Anne looks at me. I shake my head.

"Just look at them!"

"Go and get them, then," says Les.

"Yeah." Hank and I agree.

"I don't know." Anne looks at the rocks.

"Nobody's stopping you," says Les.

"There might be snakes."

"Snakes won't kill you. These snakes are just ordinary snakes," says Les.

"Then you go and get them."

"I don't like raspberries."

Ayissomaawa...Patience. Must have patience. Soon I will have them. I must have them. Must be careful. Not move. Too soon. Wait. Time. Old woman. Now old woman. Do not frighten.

"Let's go, then. You girls wait for us here. Okay?"

"Why do we have to wait?"

Hank is real nasty. "All right. If you want to walk down, I'm not stopping you."

"I'm not going any place." Anne drops to the ground. "You guys can get the horses."

Hank and Les run down the coulee.

"Do you smell something funny?" says Anne.

"Yeah, it smells like sage."

"No. Sage doesn't smell like that."

"Maybe it's dry mint."

"No. Mint doesn't smell like that, either."

"Maybe it's a snake den. Snakes like rocks, you know."

"No. It isn't snakes."

"How do you know?"

"I know," says Anne. "Now quit. You're giving me a headache."

We sit there. The sun is beating down. It is quiet. Flies drone. I feel sleepy. The sun is warm on my back.

Ayissomaawa...

"Anne! Girlie! Get over here."

Les and Hank have the horses. They wait while we bring the sack of berries.

"Come on. Hurry up!"

"I don't feel so good, Hank," says Anne. "I have a headache."

"Me too."

Hank and Les look at each other. "So do we."

"Maybe we should just go home."

"We can't let a stupid headache stop us from hunting for arrowheads."

Anne and I stand there, looking at Hank. Nobody says anything. Hank looks at us. "Just around the bend is where we found them last time."

"I wonder if there are any left," says Les.

"There should be plenty."

"What happened to the other ones we found?"

"Mom still has them. She takes them out every once in a while."

Ayissomaawa...Horses. Horses know us. Must be careful.

"Are we going to hunt arrowheads or stand around here all day?" I say.

"We're going. Now get on that horse."

Hank lifts Anne and me up on Brownie and ties the sack to his saddle. "Ready to go?"

"Yeah."

The horses walk sideways. Their ears flick back and forth. Their eyes roll, and they jerk their heads up and down. We don't go very far.

"What's that smell?"

"Smells like sage to me."

"No, it doesn't." Anne is emphatic. I agree with her.

"Well, it doesn't smell half-bad. It sure is strange, though. Wonder what's causing it." Les looks around.

"What's that?" Anne points to the rocks. I try to see over her shoulder.

"Where?"

"Over there. See?"

"It's just a shadow."

"There's something there," says Anne.

The horses balk. Hoss backs into Brownie.

"Let's go see. Let's find out what it is. Come on, Hank."

Hank licks his lips. "Do you think we should?"

We look at him.

"Well, the horses don't want to go."

Les stands up in his stirrups to get a better view. A surprised look crosses his face.

"It's an old woman."

Brownie whirls. Takes off down the side of the coulee. Anne and I hold on tight. I didn't know Brownie had that much speed. As we hit the bottom of the coulee, I see two riders loom up in front of us. Brownie stumbles, and both of us fall.

"Are you hurt?" Dad sounds worried.

"No," I say, and he pulls me off Anne.

"Anne, Anne, you all right?"

Anne lies there, trying to catch her breath. I look up and see Sam.

"Anne, you all right?"

"Yeah, Dad. I'm okay." Anne lies back and starts to cry.

Before Hank and Les can slide to a stop, Dad is already yelling. "How many times have I told you not to run the horses like that?"

"We didn't do nothing." Hank points back to the rocks. "The horses...they just took off when they saw that old lady in the coulee."

"What are you talking about?"

"An old woman...in the coulee." Hank looks at Les.

"She spooked the horses," says Les.

Dad looks back and forth, eyeing each of us. He knows we wouldn't dare lie to him.

"Did you see her?"

"We didn't get a good look," says Les.

Dad looks at us and then at Sam.

"It was near those rocks," says Hank.

"Yeah, and it smelled kinda like sage," says Les.

"You kids get home right now," says Dad. He shoves me and Anne back up on Brownie. "Get going! Stay there till I get back."

We know an order when we hear one.

Too late. Must move. Always moving. He'll come. Tired. Tired. He has power. He will come. No more.

Dad stands at the mouth of the coulee holding the two horses.

Sam walks into the coulee.

---

* **Ayissomaawa:** in the Blackfoot (Siksikaw) language,"something is near," with the connotation that it is something dangerous

* **coulee:** in western Canada, a deep ravine that is dry in summer

* **wolverine:** an animal related not to the wolf but to the weasel, with extremely powerful jaws, small head and large, rounded back. It secretes a strong-smelling fluid, especially when frightened or about to attack; the smell may cause headaches in some people

A Question Mark And An Exclamation Point

REVAZ MISHVELADZE

L et no man claim, *batono*,* that he knows people. A person can sometimes pull such a stunt that afterward he himself won't be able to make head or tail of his actions—and somebody else, of course, will understand them all the less. For this reason, you know, nothing surprises me in this world. You can't guess ahead of time how your own friend will behave and what he'll do. Now, apropos of that, I was in court recently, heard the case of some people I know pretty well. Well, did they lay it on thick—not only did nobody expect it of them, but when the indictment was read we couldn't believe our ears. A lawyer, you'll say, a lawyer can figure people out, surely he, a lawyer, knows what's what. No, *batono*, a thousand times no: a lawyer is a person just like you and me. It's not granted to him to peer into the very depths of the human soul, its innermost recesses, and besides, he doesn't have the time for it. You must believe me—not a single clairvoyant can penetrate the thickets of the soul of Adam's son.* An investigator is armed with the beacon of the law and supposedly with its help lights up the hidden passages in that very soul. The only thing is, he can't go a step further than the law stipulates, he's limited and bound by the law. And, after all, human deeds and actions cannot by any means always be reduced to law or lawlessness! Man, *batono*, is an unfathomable, confused, enigmatic creature. Yes, and then there are the psychologists, who pretend to a knowledge of the psyche, that is, the soul; only it's empty talk, don't believe them, they don't understand a smidgen about it. Some of them claim that instinct rules man's actions, others shout—no, it isn't instinct, but reason, reason is the origin of everything, while still others declare it's both reason and besides that—genes. That's how it is. But there are actions, after all, that don't submit to any logic, and the motives for which are beyond understanding. If you take things on the whole, abstractly, then wherever they might lead you can still kind of define them and put them in their proper cubbyholes, but when it comes to something concrete you get tangled up and squirm like a mouse in a trap. But what am I doing talking about other people, trying to fathom others? Let me tell you about myself. And if I am lying even the slightest bit, may my enemy be struck dead.

At the time this incident took place I was just under thirty. It's a well-known fact that at that age a man is no longer a child. I lived upstairs, you know, on Uritsky Street—I was renting a room in the cobbler Dzhikia's house and was working in Mtsvanekvavila* at a brick factory. It was a tiny little room—I got married late, you know, I was still a bachelor at the time, and besides, I was short of funds and therefore tried to spend as little as I could. Well, even though the room was tiny, it had a window facing the street, it was sunny and dry.... And besides, I had no need for a big room. The little tin stove heated mine up right away even in the bitterest cold, and during the summer heat waves I spent almost all my evenings at Rioni;* I swam, splashed about—in a word, kept cool. While in the wintertime I would run in from work, light the stove, and tumble into bed—I'd relish the warmth and rest.

One fine evening—I remember it as if it were yesterday, it was New Year's, old style*—I was sitting by my stove listening to the droning of the wind. It was cold outside, a north wind was kicking up its heels. Suddenly somebody knocked at my door. It wasn't very late yet, it had just recently gotten dark. In the winter, you know yourself, before you have time to turn around it's already dark. Who could it be? I thought. However, unlike others, who are forever asking "Who's there?" I never ask. God is my witness, for good or ill, whenever someone knocks at my door (it's true even now, at my considerable age) I go to the door and open it without thinking twice. And so I opened the door and on the threshold stood our police inspector, Morgoshia. A round-faced sort of fellow, thickset, always full of smiles. The two of us had chatted a couple of times. He had shown up for the first time when I had just settled into this room. He wrote down who I was, what I was, then we split a jug of *tsolikauri** and parted quite pleased with each other. Since then we exchanged a very friendly hello whenever we met, and that was all. What brought him, what kind of business does he have with me? I thought.

Morgoshia opened his folder, pulled out a paper, and silently held it out to me. "What's the matter?" I said. "A neighbor has a complaint." Which neighbor could it be, what neighbor, whom did I offend, and how? I live quietly, peaceably, like a bug in a rug....

I began reading the complaint and just plain broke out in a sweat. But when I had read it to the end I just didn't know what to say. First laughter grabbed me, then, after I looked at Morgoshia and saw his unusually serious round face, I also tried to put on a serious expression, but there was no way I could gather my lips together—they kept spreading into a smile.

What do you think, what was I accused of?

Beyond the wall, in the other, neighboring half of the house, there lived a certain Ucha Chumburidze. A solitary man like me. At that time he must have been a little over fifty. I don't know if he's still alive.... He was a squat, stout man with a big head and an immense birthmark on his forehead. He was a hatter, it seems. He went out of the house extremely rarely. As long as I had lived there, I hadn't spoken to him once. I had nothing to do with him, nor he with me. Besides, the entrance to that half of the house was on another street. Our courtyard, I should mention, was partitioned in two: my landlord and this same Chumburidze had each built half the house, then a quarrel had broken out between them and they stopped talking to each other. And so it was none other than Chumburidze who was making a complaint against me: such-and-such, says he (it turned out that he knew both my first name and my last, and where I worked!), climbs up to the attic in the middle of the night, crawls across to my side, moves aside the attic trapdoor, and looks into my room from there. I ask you to ascertain, he addressed the police, what he wants from me.

"What, are all his screws loose or something?" I asked Morgoshia.

"All I've got to worry about is looking at his birthmark, for that I even climb up to the attic, right? Come on, what nonsense!"

Nevertheless, Morgoshia examined my room, then went out to the gallery, stared at the ceiling, and—"Where," he said, "is the exit to the attic?" "How should I know?" I said, frowning. "What would I be doing in the attic, am I a chimney sweep?" That half-wit Chumburidze makes up heaven knows what, and you, Morgoshia, get it into your head to check me out for real, is that it?" "Why, no," he said, "I have no particular reason, I'm interested for myself. I have to look into this business, you know, so I can explain to the man that he was dreaming."

Well, all right, he and I went down to the courtyard. An iron staircase there ran along the blank brick wall of the house to the garret roof. To tell the truth, I hadn't even noticed it before, that staircase. So, it meant that in such freezing cold, at night, I was supposed to have gone out into the courtyard, climbed the iron staircase to the roof—in the dark, mind you—made my way along the tin gutter to Chumburidze's attic, crept in there, found the trapdoor, moved it aside, and—contemplated the hatter's blackhead-speckled, idiotic face!...

Morgoshia, like a tried-and-true detective, examined everything in detail and, with me at his side, clambered up to the attic, lighting the way with his flashlight. And, after convincing himself that not only in the past few days, but even in the past five years, no one had set foot there (the dust all around was a finger thick—if anyone had walked on it, he would have left footprints as deep as those Armstrong and his colleague had left on the moon), he and I silently climbed back down.

"The devil take that Chumburidze," he muttered when we were at last standing on the ground. "Making us swallow all that dust! All I needed were his fantasies! Well, all right, go ahead and get a good night's sleep. I'll unscramble his brains for him, I'll show him what it means to make up some cock-and-bull story about a person."

The inspector's visit to me, of course, didn't escape the notice of my landlord's family. As one they all spilled out onto the balcony and silently, raptly, observed our stroll to the roof. They also heard Morgoshia's concluding speech, but went into the house without saying a word, without asking me about anything. It was plain to see they knew what an oddball our precious neighbor was.

Meanwhile, Morgoshia came out on the street, rounded our courtyard, and went in Chumburidze's gate. I don't know what they talked about, only Morgoshia didn't leave there for a long time. I was about to go to bed when I suddenly heard loud voices. I opened the window, listened.

"You should see a doctor, a doctor!" Morgoshia said, exasperated.

"I don't need to see a doctor! You're barking up the wrong tree! You better quit making such statements, or else you'll be stripped of your rank!" Ucha said, not giving in.

Morgoshia stood in the middle of the courtyard.

"What can I answer? I don't have the right to get mixed up with you, I'm here on duty! The tongue is loose, it can say anything. But you leave him in peace, he has troubles enough of his own without having to deal with your fantasies. He doesn't have anything to do with your ceiling," Morgoshia answered him very reasonably. And on that it ended—the inspector left.

The next morning I went to work as usual and, to tell the truth, I forgot about the incident, not having attached much importance to it. Well, I thought, it happens, a person imagines some absurd thing; maybe he was in a bad mood, or what have you. The hell with him.

One day passed; the second day nothing happened either. On the third, as soon as it grew dark, Morgoshia appeared once again.

"We just barely calmed your neighbor down," Morgoshia said. "He came this afternoon and claimed you peeped in at him twice yesterday from the ceiling. I was about to pipe up about visions and dreams, but he flew into such a rage. 'You,' he said, 'think I'm crazy, a psycho, but he and I'—he meant you—'looked at each other yesterday just like we are doing right now. What,' he said, 'does he want from me, what's he staring at me for? If I'm a psycho,' he said, 'why don't I imagine other things, why don't I attack people on the street, huh? This is already the fourth night that he's been gawking into my room from the ceiling, he doesn't give me a moment's peace.' Then I said to him, 'Board up that damned door, and that'll be the end of it, you'll get some peace.' 'I already boarded it up,' he said, 'and he tore it off! How can I get rid of him—it's beyond me!' 'But he's not a bird, you know, he can't fly,' I said. 'So how come he doesn't leave footprints anywhere?' But there's no way of getting through to Chumburidze, he keeps repeating the same thing, until you could burst," Morgoshia related rapidly, almost gasping, with bulging eyes and puffed-out cheeks.

"What in the world should I do now?" I asked.

"Write that Chumburidze is slandering you, that the thought of climbing up to his attic never even crossed your mind, that your attitude toward him is good, neighborly. That you harbor no evil against him in either head or heart, and that for the entire time you've been living here you haven't said as much as a nasty word to each other," Morgoshia advised me.

I wrote down everything just as he said. Morgoshia took my statement and left. And I got into bed without even eating supper, thinking that if I didn't come up with something the next day, that raving Chumburidze would have me under his thumb once and for all.

And it was at that very moment that the inexplicable and improbable thing happened inside me, which is the reason I've been telling you this story in the first place.

I was lying down and sleep didn't come—what am I saying, sleep? I wasn't even getting drowsy. I was tossing and turning. And Chumburidze's sour puss with its swollen eyes and that birthmark on his forehead loomed before me.

What does he want from me? I thought. Why is he pestering me and spreading all that nonsense to boot? There's no doubt about it, he is imagining something, but what does it have to do with me? And what if I went to him right now and said, "Let's talk things over man to man, without any ifs, ands, or buts, what do you have against me, why have you blackened my name?..." But what if he decides that I've come to attack him and lets out a scream or, worse still, lands me one on the head with a stick? You can expect anything you like from his type. And what if I make a complaint against him? I'll say he's slandering me, I can't go on living like this. Well, who knows what would come of it.... My case has already begun, Morgoshia knows me, but a new investigator would start interrogating and pumping me, "Who are you, why have you come, how much do you pay for your room?..." All these questions wouldn't do either me or Dzhikia any good at all.... Still, I'd like to know what that screwball hatter does at night, why he's so afraid of somebody seeing him. No, there's definitely something shady going on, no two ways about it. As for me, for instance, I don't care, go ahead and peep in at me if you want. It doesn't worry me at all. I wonder if he's sleeping now or not? Most likely he's sitting and gaping at the ceiling. What if I really did peep in on him—what would his expression be then?

I don't remember how I jumped out of bed and got dressed, how I went out to the courtyard. I was driven by an irresistible urge to peep from the ceiling into Ucha Chumburidze's room, to see his bewildered face and find out what it was he did nights. With great difficulty I climbed up the iron staircase, crawled as stealthily as a cat across the garret to Chumburidze's half of the roof, made my way into the attic, gropingly found the trapdoor, and, the very instant I moved it aside, encountered the bulging eyes of the crazed hatter and heard an inhuman howl:

"Morgoshia, save me!"

"I'm here!" barked Morgoshia almost right above my ear, whereupon Ucha cried in a triumphant voice:

"What, am I imagining things now too? Are you going to say I'm dreaming again?"

Then steps began to stomp and rumble about the attic, a flashlight shone on my back, and I heard Morgoshia's voice:

"Don't move or I'll shoot!"

After a short pause the inspector declared peremptorily:

"Climb out on the roof and go down the staircase, I'll be waiting for you below."

Only when I was climbing down the staircase, ashamed and disheartened, did it occur to me what a mess I had made. Until then some mysterious, insuperable force had guided me.

I was greeted below by Morgoshia, my landlord's entire large family, Chumburidze with a cast-iron frying pan in his hands, and a police car.

My first testimony turned out to be so confused, tangled, and inconsistent that the Lord God Himself couldn't have made sense of what I had wanted in the attic. Then somebody took pity and prompted me: Say it was a joke, that you just wanted to give him a good scare. To make a long story short, my case was turned over to a comrades' court*. I was fined fifty rubles and had to sign a statement that from then on I would never allow myself any "jokes" of that kind.

It was out of the question, of course, for me to go on living in that house. The very next day I gathered my belongings and settled my account with the landlord. And a couple of months later I also bade farewell to the brick factory and moved to Tkibuli*.

* **batono:** sir, mister
* **Adam's son:** refers to all human beings, male and female
* **Mtsvanekvavila:** a suburb of Kutaisi, a small Georgian town near the Black Sea
* **Rioni:** a small resort area on the Black Sea
* **New Year's, old style:** in certain parts of the Soviet Union, people celebrate the new year twice: once on January 1, and again on January 13, the date when the new year occurred in the old Julian calendar

* **tsolikauri:** wine
* **comrades' court:** a local court composed of members of the Communist party as well as a few of the accused's neighbours; it dealt with minor offences
* **Tkibuli:** a small town outside of Kutaisi

As the Buffaloes Bathed

PRETAM KAUR

There was a man who wanted to die but could not. Death seemed to have forgotten him completely and was busy elsewhere. Life had made him sick, given him a sickness which swelled his legs and aged him. Small boys said that he had legs like an elephant's but not as strong. He was sick for a long time, for long years, and people almost forgot him. He became a memory for no one saw him for ages on his elephant legs.

But his family could not forget him. There he lay on his bed for years, and the family ran round in circles tending to his needs. They ran round in circles and bumped into each other and went crazy looking after him. They became giddy looking after him, and they all aged with pain, even the youngest. And the man became hollow, became empty, just a shell, with swollen legs—so sick that there was nothing anyone could do. He grew querulous and mad, and he picked on his family and tore them to pieces in his frenzy of frustration and they aged with hurt and pain. He wanted death, but death had forgotten him and remembered instead a five-year-old in a pond, a thirty-five-year-old on a Honda, and others who did not want to go. But she forgot this man who was ready.

"Take me to Sumitry's house, I want to go there. I don't want to stay here any more, I don't like it here. Take me to Sumitry's house," the man wailed night and day with this new idea in his head.

"Man, how can we do that, what would Sumitry's in-laws think? Have some sense of shame. You can't squat in Sumitry's place like this," the woman said.

But no, he would not give up his new idea, he must go to Sumitry's place.

So Sumitry took him to her place and took care of him in earnest, in her love. She ran round in circles caring for him, answering his calls. Her in-laws were nice and understood, but how long can understanding last before exhaustion sets in?

"I want to go to Raju's house. Take me to Raju's house. I don't like it here anymore, I want to go to Raju's house," the man began to say with another new idea in his head.

Raju was the son and it was safe to go there. So they took him to Raju's house.

The years went by, and at the end of each year he was still there. His wife became a stick, his daughters lost their glow and became dull-eyed, and his sons walked as if with loads on their backs. They ran in circles and became giddy with running. And at last began to pray "Dear God...." It is a prayer no one ever wishes to say—or say out loud—but now they began in their anguish to say "Dear God..." and pray. And still he was forgotten.

Now he wanted to go, he was ready, his bags were packed. He said, "I'm only waiting for the train to come." But trains like some deaths can be slow and he waited. And they waited, though they never said so.

In their exhaustion, one hot afternoon, they all laid their tired heads on pillows. The house was still, no one was about, and the gate was open. The man got up, took his walking stick and shuffled out, silently as if on a cloud. And they slept on with their tired heads on pillows that long hot afternoon.

When they awoke he was gone. Look for him in the kitchen, in the bathroom, under the bed, he was nowhere. Look outside, behind, in the drain, but he was nowhere. Ask the neighbours, did you see our old man? No, they had not seen him. Where could he be? Shall we call the police, has he been kidnapped, or lost? And the family ran here and ran there, in circles, not knowing where to run, where to look, for they didn't know where he could have gone. He had lost contact with the outside world for ten years. There was no friend he could be visiting, no crony he could be with, no favourite haunts he could return to. Ten years make a lot of difference to people and scenes. And the family did not know where to look for him. But they did run around, frantic everywhere, looking for him and telling everyone else to do the same.

He had walked silently out and down the road, and no one saw him because no one knew him. He was just a man shuffling on the road on a burning afternoon. His mind at last remembered one place, remembered it from ten years ago. Yes, he must go there, that was the place. That couldn't have changed for you can't really build on a lake where the buffaloes bathed. And his mind guided him there, and people passed him on the way and took no notice but later they remembered. Yes, they had seen a man, the only walking man in the hot afternoon. And he came to the lake—and it was there as his mind had told him. The lazy water made small waves, and in the far distance little Indian boys fished under the shade. He remembered the place, and death remembered him—at last. And the man walked into the lake and put his nose down into the muddy water in the hot afternoon, as the buffaloes bathed.

A Very Old Man With Enormous Wings

GABRIEL GARCÍA MÁRQUEZ

On the third day of rain they had killed so many crabs inside the house that Pelayo had to cross his drenched courtyard and throw them into the sea, because the newborn child had a temperature all night and they thought it was due to the stench. The world had been sad since Tuesday. Sea and sky were a single ash-gray thing and the sands of the beach, which on March nights glimmered like powdered light, had become a stew of mud and rotten shellfish. The light was so weak at noon that when Pelayo was coming back to the house after throwing away the crabs, it was hard for him to see what it was that was moving and groaning in the rear of the courtyard. He had to go very close to see that it was an old man, a very old man, lying face down in the mud, who, in spite of his tremendous efforts, couldn't get up, impeded by his enormous wings.

Frightened by that nightmare, Pelayo ran to get Elisenda, his wife, who was putting compresses on the sick child, and he took her to the rear of the courtyard. They both looked at the fallen body with mute stupor. He was dressed like a ragpicker. There were only a few faded hairs left on his bald skull and very few teeth in his mouth, and his pitiful condition of a drenched great-grandfather had taken away any sense of grandeur he might have had. His huge buzzard wings, dirty and half-plucked, were forever entangled in the mud. They looked at him so long and so closely that Pelayo and Elisenda overcame their surprise and in the end found him familiar. Then they dared speak to him, and he answered in an incomprehensible dialect with a strong sailor's voice. That was how they skipped over the inconvenience of the wings and quite intelligently concluded that he was a lonely castaway from some foreign ship wrecked by a storm. And yet, they called in a neighbor woman who knew everything about life and death to see him, and all she needed was one look to show them their mistake.

"He's an angel," she told them. "He must have been coming for the child, but the poor fellow is so old that the rain knocked him down."

On the following day everyone knew that a flesh-and-blood angel was held captive in Pelayo's house. Against the judgment of the wise neighbor woman, for whom angels in those times were the fugitive survivors of a celestial conspiracy, they did not have the heart to club him to death. Pelayo watched over him all afternoon from the kitchen, armed with his bailiff's club, and before going to bed he dragged him out of the mud and locked him up with the hens in the wire chicken coop. In the middle of the night, when the rain stopped, Pelayo and Elisenda were still killing crabs. A short time afterward the child woke up without a fever and with a desire to eat. Then they felt magnanimous and decided to put the angel on a raft with fresh water and provisions for three days and leave him to his fate on the high seas. But when they went out into the courtyard with the first light of dawn, they found the whole neighborhood in front of the chicken coop having fun with the angel, without the slightest reverence, tossing him things to eat through the openings in the wire as if he weren't a supernatural creature but a circus animal.

Father Gonzaga arrived before seven o'clock, quite alarmed at the strange news. By that time onlookers less frivolous than those at dawn had already arrived and they were making all kinds of conjectures concerning the captive's future. The simplest among them thought that he should be named mayor of the world. Others of sterner mind felt that he should be promoted to the rank of five-star general in order to win all wars. Some visionaries hoped that he could be put to stud in order to implant on earth a race of winged wise men who could take charge of the universe. But Father Gonzaga, before becoming a priest, had been a robust woodcutter. Standing by the wire, he reviewed his catechism* in an instant and asked them to open the door so that he could take a close look at that pitiful man who looked more like a decrepit hen among the fascinated chickens. He was lying in a corner drying his open wings in the sunlight among the fruit peels and breakfast leftovers that the early risers had thrown him. Alien to the impertinences of the world, he only lifted his antiquarian eyes and murmured something in his dialect when Father Gonzaga went into the chicken coop and said good morning to him in Latin. The parish priest had his first suspicion of an imposter when he saw that he did not understand the language of God* or know how to greet His ministers. Then he noticed that seen up close he was much too human: he had an unbearable smell of the outdoors, the back side of his wings were strewn with parasites and his main feathers had been mistreated by terrestrial winds, and nothing about him measured up to the proud dignity of angels. Then he came out of the chicken coop and in a brief sermon warned the curious against the risks of being ingenuous. He reminded them that the devil had the bad habit of making use of carnival tricks in order to confuse the unwary. He argued that if wings were not the essential element in determining the difference between a hawk and an airplane, they were even less so in the recognition of angels. Nevertheless, he promised to write a letter to his bishop* so that the latter would write to his primate so that the latter would write to the Supreme Pontiff* in order to get the final verdict from the highest courts.

His prudence fell on sterile hearts. The news of the captive angel spread with such rapidity that after a few hours the courtyard had the bustle of a marketplace and they had to call in the troops with fixed bayonets to disperse the mob that was about to knock the house down. Elisenda, her spine all twisted from sweeping up so much marketplace trash, then got the idea of fencing in the yard and charging five cents admission to see the angel.

The curious came from far away. A traveling carnival arrived with a flying acrobat who buzzed over the crowd several times, but no one paid any attention to him because his wings were not those of an angel but, rather, those of a sidereal bat. The most unfortunate invalids on earth came in search of health: a poor woman who since childhood had been counting her heartbeats and had run out of numbers; a Portuguese man who couldn't sleep because the noise of the stars disturbed him; a sleepwalker who got up at night to undo the things he had done while awake; and many others with less serious ailments. In the midst of that shipwreck disorder that made the earth tremble, Pelayo and Elisenda were happy with fatigue, for in less than a week they had crammed their rooms with money and the line of pilgrims waiting their turn to enter still reached beyond the horizon.

The angel was the only one who took no part in his own act. He spent his time trying to get comfortable in his borrowed nest, befuddled by the hellish heat of the oil lamps and sacramental candles that had been placed along the wire. At first they tried to make him eat mothballs, which, according to the wisdom of the wise neighbor woman, were the food prescribed for angels. But he turned them down, just as he turned down the papal lunches that the penitents brought him, and they never found out whether it was because he was an angel or because he was an old man that in the end he ate nothing but eggplant mush. His only supernatural virtue seemed to be patience. Especially during the first days, when the hens pecked at him, searching for the stellar parasites that proliferated in his wings, and the cripples pulled out feathers to touch their defective parts with, and even the most merciful threw stones at him, trying to get him to rise so they could see him standing. The only time they succeeded in arousing him was when they burned his side with an iron for branding steers, for he had been motionless for so many hours that they thought he was dead. He awoke with a start, ranting in his hermetic language and with tears in his eyes, and he flapped his wings a couple of times, which brought on a whirlwind of chicken dung and lunar dust and a gale of panic that did not seem to be of this world. Although many thought that his reaction had not been one of rage but of pain, from then on they were careful not to annoy him, because the majority understood that his passivity was not that of a hero taking his ease but that of a cataclysm in repose.

Father Gonzaga held back the crowd's frivolity with formulas of maidservant inspiration while awaiting the arrival of a final judgment on the nature of the captive. But the mail from Rome* showed no sense of urgency. They spent their time finding out if the prisoner had a navel, if his dialect had any connection with Aramaic,* how many times he could fit on the head of a pin, or whether he wasn't just a Norwegian with wings. Those meagre letters might have come and gone until the end of time if a providential event had not put an end to the priest's tribulations.

It so happened that during those days, among so many other carnival attractions, there arrived in town the traveling show of a woman who had been changed into a spider for having disobeyed her parents. The admission to see her was not only less than the admission to see the angel, but people were permitted to ask her all manner of questions about her absurd state and to examine her up and down so that no one would ever doubt the truth of her horror. She was a frightful tarantula the size of a ram with the head of a sad maiden. What was most heartrending, however, was not her outlandish shape but the most sincere affliction with which she recounted the details of her misfortune. While still practically a child she had sneaked out of her parents' house to go to a dance, and while she was coming back through the woods after having danced all night without permission, a fearful thunderclap rent the sky in two and through the crack came the lightning bolt of brimstone that changed her into a spider. Her only nourishment came from the meatballs that charitable souls chose to toss into her mouth. A spectacle like that, full of so much human truth and with such a fearful lesson, was bound to defeat without even trying that of a haughty angel who scarcely deigned to look at mortals. Besides, the few miracles attributed to the angel showed a certain mental disorder, like the blind man who didn't recover his sight but grew three new teeth, or the paralytic who didn't get to walk but almost won the lottery, and the leper whose sores sprouted sunflowers. Those consolation miracles, which were more like mocking fun, had already ruined the angel's reputation when the woman who had been changed into a spider finally crushed him completely. That was how Father Gonzaga was cured forever of his insomnia and Pelayo's courtyard went back to being as empty as during the time it rained for three days and crabs walked through the bedrooms.

The owners of the house had no reason to lament. With the money they saved they built a two-storey mansion with balconies and gardens and high netting so that crabs wouldn't get in during the winter, and with iron bars on the windows so that angels wouldn't get in. Pelayo also set up a rabbit warren close to town and gave up his job as bailiff for good, and Elisenda bought some satin pumps with high heels and many dresses of iridescent silk, the kind worn on Sunday by the most desirable women in those times. The chicken coop was the only thing that didn't receive any attention. If they washed it down with creolin and burned tears of myrrh inside it every so often, it was not in homage to the angel but to drive away the dungheap stench that still hung everywhere like a ghost and was turning the new house into an old one. At first, when the child learned to walk, they were careful that he not get too close to the chicken coop. But then they began to lose their fears and got used to the smell, and before the child got his second teeth he'd gone inside the chicken coop to play, where the wires were falling apart. The angel was no less standoffish with him than with other mortals, but he tolerated the most ingenious infamies with the patience of a dog who had no illusions. They both came down with chicken pox at the same time. The doctor who took care of the child couldn't resist the temptation to listen to the angel's heart, and he found so much whistling in the heart and so many sounds in his kidneys that it seemed impossible for him to be alive. What surprised him most, however, was the logic of his wings. They seemed so natural on that completely human organism that he couldn't understand why other men didn't have them too.

When the child began school it had been some time since the sun and rain had caused the collapse of the chicken coop. The angel went dragging himself about here and there like a stray dying man. They would drive him out of the bedroom with a broom and a moment later find him in the kitchen. He seemed to be in so many places at the same time that they grew to think that he had been duplicated, that he was reproducing himself all through the house, and the exasperated and unhinged Elisenda shouted that it was awful living in that hell of angels. He could scarcely eat and his antiquarian eyes had become so foggy that he went about bumping into posts. All he had left were the bare cannulae* of his last feathers. Pelayo threw a blanket over him and extended him the charity of letting him sleep in the shed, and only then did they notice that he had a temperature at night, and was delirious with the tongue twisters of an old Norwegian. That was one of the few times they became alarmed, for they thought he was going to die and not even the wise neighbor woman had been able to tell them what to do with dead angels.

And yet he not only survived his worst winter, but seemed improved with the first sunny days. He remained motionless for several days in the farthest corner of the courtyard, where no one would see him, and at the beginning of December some large, stiff feathers began to grow on his wings, the feathers of a scarecrow, which looked more like another misfortune of decrepitude. But he must have known the reason for those changes, for he was quite careful that no one should notice them, that no one should hear the sea chanteys that he sometimes sang under the stars. One morning Elisenda was cutting some bunches of onions for lunch when a wind that seemed to come from the high seas blew into the kitchen. Then she went to the window and caught the angel in his first attempts at flight. They were so clumsy that his fingernails opened a furrow in the vegetable patch and he was on the point of knocking the shed down with the ungainly flapping that couldn't get a grip on the air. But he did manage to gain altitude. Elisenda let out a sigh of relief, for herself and for him, when she saw him pass over the last houses, holding himself up in some way with the risky flapping of a senile vulture. She kept watching him even when she was through cutting the onions and she kept on watching until it was no longer possible for her to see him, because then he was no longer an annoyance in her life but an imaginary dot on the horizon of the sea.

* **catechism:** instruction, by question and answer, for religious purposes

* **language of God:** here, Latin, the language of the ancient Romans, and the language in which the Roman Catholic church until recently conducted its services

* **bishop:** overseer or elder in religious community; here, Roman Catholic primate

* **Supreme Pontiff:** the Pope, head of the Roman Catholic church

* **Rome:** capital of Italy; here, synonymous with the Pope

* **Aramaic:** ancient language of the Middle East, current in the time of Jesus

* **cannulae:** medical: a small tube inserted into the skin to allow fluid to escape; here, the small tubes at the base of the old man's feathers

Day of the Butterfly

ALICE MUNRO

I do not remember when Myra Sayla came to town, though she must have been in our class at school for two or three years. I start remembering her in the last year, when her little brother Jimmy Sayla was in Grade One. Jimmy Sayla was not used to going to the bathroom by himself and he would have to come to the Grade Six door and ask for Myra and she would take him downstairs. Quite often he would not get to Myra in time and there would be a big dark stain on his little button-on cotton pants. Then Myra had to come and ask the teacher: "Please may I take my brother home, he has wet himself?"

That was what she said the first time and everybody in the front seats heard her—though Myra's voice was the lightest singsong—and there was a muted giggling which alerted the rest of the class. Our teacher, a cold gentle girl who wore glasses with thin gold rims and in the stiff solicitude of certain poses resembled a giraffe, wrote something on a piece of paper and showed it to Myra. And Myra recited uncertainly: "My brother has had an accident, please, teacher."

Everybody knew of Jimmy Sayla's shame and at recess (if he was not being kept in, as he often was, for doing something he shouldn't in school) he did not dare go out on the school grounds, where the other little boys, and some bigger ones, were waiting to chase him and corner him against the back fence and thrash him with tree branches. He had to stay with Myra. But at our school there were the two sides, the Boys' Side and the Girls' Side, and it was believed that if you so much as stepped on the side that was not your own you might easily get the strap. Jimmy could not go out on the Girls' Side and Myra could not go out on the Boys' Side, and no one was allowed to stay in the school unless it was raining or snowing. So Myra and Jimmy spent every recess standing in the little back porch between the two sides. Perhaps they watched the baseball games, the tag and skipping and building of leaf houses in the fall and snow forts in the winter; perhaps they did not watch at all. Whenever you happened to look at them their heads were slightly bent, their narrow bodies hunched in, quite still. They had long smooth oval faces, melancholy and discreet—dark, oily, shining hair. The little boy's was long, clipped at home, and Myra's was worn in heavy braids coiled on top of her head so that she looked, from a distance, as if she was wearing a turban too big for her. Over their dark eyes the lids were never fully raised; they had a weary look. But it was more than that. They were like children in a medieval painting, they were like small figures carved of wood, for worship or magic, with faces smooth and aged, and meekly, cryptically uncommunicative.

Most of the teachers at our school had been teaching for a long time and at recess they would disappear into the teachers' room and not bother us. But our own teacher, the young woman of the fragile gold-rimmed glasses, was apt to watch us from a window and sometimes come out, looking brisk and uncomfortable, to stop a fight among the little girls or start a running game among the big ones, who had been huddled together playing Truth or Secrets. One day she came out and called, "Girls in Grade Six, I want to talk to you!" She smiled persuasively, earnestly, and with dreadful unease, showing fine gold rims around her teeth. She said, "There is a girl in Grade Six called Myra Sayla. She *is* in your grade, isn't she?"

We mumbled. But there was a coo from Gladys Healey. "Yes, Miss Darling!"

"Well, why is she never playing with the rest of you? Every day I see her standing in the back porch, never playing. Do you think she looks very happy standing back there? Do you think you would be very happy, if *you* were left back there?"

Nobody answered; we faced Miss Darling, all respectful, self-possessed, and bored with the unreality of her question. Then Gladys said, "Myra can't come out with us, Miss Darling. Myra has to look after her little brother!"

"Oh," said Miss Darling dubiously. "Well you ought to try to be nicer to her anyway. Don't you think so? Don't you? You will try to be nicer, won't you? I *know* you will." Poor Miss Darling! Her campaigns were soon confused, her persuasions turned to bleating and uncertain pleas.

When she had gone Gladys Healey said softly, "You will try to be nicer, won't you? I *know* you will!" and then drawing her lip back over her big teeth she yelled exuberantly, "I don't care if it rains or freezes." She went through the whole verse and ended it with a spectacular twirl of her Royal Stuart tartan skirt. Mr. Healey ran a Dry Goods and Ladies' Wear, and his daughter's leadership in our class was partly due to her flashing plaid skirts and organdie blouses and velvet jackets with brass buttons, but also to her early-maturing bust and the fine brutal force of her personality. Now we all began to imitate Miss Darling.

We had not paid much attention to Myra before this. But now a game was developed; it started with saying, "Let's be nice to Myra!" Then we would walk up to her in formal groups of three or four and at a signal, say together, "Hel-lo Myra, Hello *My*-ra!" and follow up with something like, "What do you wash your hair in, Myra, it's so nice and shiny, My-ra." "Oh she washes it in cod-liver oil, don't you, Myra, she washes it in cod-liver oil, can't you smell it?"

And to tell the truth there was a smell about Myra, but it was a rotten-sweetish smell as of bad fruit. That was what the Saylas did, kept a little fruit store. Her father sat all day on a stool by the window, with his shirt open over his swelling stomach and tufts of black hair showing around his belly button; he chewed garlic. But if you went into the store it was Mrs. Sayla who came to wait on you, appearing silently between the limp print curtains hung across the back of the store. Her hair was crimped in black waves and she smiled with her full lips held together, stretched as far as they would go; she told you the price in a little rapping voice, daring you to challenge her and, when you did not, handed you the bag of fruit with open mockery in her eyes.

One morning in the winter I was walking up the school hill very early; a neighbour had given me a ride into town. I lived about half a mile out of town, on a farm, and I should not have been going to the town school at all, but to a country school nearby where there were half a dozen pupils and a teacher a little demented since her change of life. But my mother, who was an ambitious woman, had prevailed on the town trustees to accept me and my father to pay the extra tuition, and I went to school in town. I was the only one in the class who carried a lunch pail and ate peanut-butter sandwiches in the high, bare, mustard-coloured cloakroom, the only one who had to wear rubber boots in the spring, when the roads were heavy with mud. I felt a little danger, on account of this; but I could not tell exactly what it was.

I saw Myra and Jimmy ahead of me on the hill; they always went to school very early—sometimes so early that they had to stand outside waiting for the janitor to open the door. They were walking slowly, and now and then Myra half turned around. I had often loitered in that way, wanting to walk with some important girl who was behind me, and not quite daring to stop and wait. Now it occurred to me that Myra might be doing this with me. I did not know what to do. I could not afford to be seen walking with her, and I did not even want to—but, on the other hand, the flattery of those humble, hopeful turnings was not lost on me. A role was shaping for me that I could not resist playing. I felt a great pleasurable rush of self-conscious benevolence; before I thought what I was doing I called, "Myra! Hey, Myra, wait up, I got some Cracker Jack!" and I quickened my pace as she stopped.

Myra waited, but she did not look at me; she waited in the withdrawn and rigid attitude with which she always met us. Perhaps she thought I was playing a trick on her, perhaps she expected me to run past and throw an empty Cracker Jack box in her face. And I opened the box and held it out to her. She took a little. Jimmy ducked behind her coat and would not take any when I offered the box to him.

"He's shy," I said reassuringly. "A lot of little kids are shy like that. He'll probably grow out of it."

"Yes," said Myra.

"I have a brother four," I said. "He's awfully shy." He wasn't. "Have some more Cracker Jack," I said. "I used to eat Cracker Jack all the time but I don't any more. I think it's bad for your complexion."

There was a silence.

"Do you like Art?" said Myra faintly.

"No. I like Social Studies and Spelling and Health."

"I like Art and Arithmetic." Myra could add and multiply in her head faster than anyone else in the class.

"I wish I was as good as you. In Arithmetic," I said, and felt magnanimous.

"But I am no good at Spelling," said Myra. "I make the most mistakes, I'll fail maybe." She did not sound unhappy about this, but pleased to have such a thing to say. She kept her head turned away from me staring at the dirty snowbanks along Victoria Street, and as she talked she made a sound as if she was wetting her lips with her tongue.

"You won't fail," I said. "You are too good in Arithmetic. What are you going to be when you grow up?"

She looked bewildered. "I will help my mother," she said. "And work in the store."

"Well I am going to be an airplane hostess," I said. "But don't mention it to anybody. I haven't told many people."

"No, I won't," said Myra. "Do you read Steve Canyon in the paper?"

"Yes." It was queer to think that Myra, too, read the comics, or that she did anything at all, apart from her role at the school. "Do you read Rip Kirby?"

"Do you read Orphan Annie?"

"Do you read Betsy and the Boys?"

"You haven't had hardly any Cracker Jack," I said. "Have some. Take a whole handful."

Myra looked into the box. "There's a prize in there," she said. She pulled it out. It was a brooch, a little tin butterfly, painted gold with bits of coloured glass stuck onto it to look like jewels. She held it in her brown hand, smiling slightly.

I said, "Do you like that?"

Myra said, "I like them blue stones. Blue stones are sapphires."

"I know. My birthstone is sapphire. What is your birthstone?"

"I don't know."

"When is your birthday?"

"July."

"Then yours is ruby."

"I like sapphire better," said Myra. "I like yours." She handed me the brooch.

"You keep it," I said. "Finders keepers."

Myra kept holding it out, as if she did not know what I meant. "Finders keepers," I said.

"It was your Cracker Jack," said Myra, scared and solemn. "You bought it."

"Well you found it."

"No—" said Myra.

"Go on!" I said. "Here, I'll *give* it to you." I took the brooch from her and pushed it back into her hand.

We were both surprised. We looked at each other; I flushed but Myra did not. I realized the pledge as our fingers touched; I was panicky, but *all right*. I thought, I can come early and walk with her other mornings, I can go and talk to her at recess. Why not? *Why not?*

Myra put the brooch in her pocket. She said, "I can wear it on my good dress. My good dress is blue."

I knew it would be. Myra wore out her good dresses at school. Even in midwinter among the plaid wool skirts and serge tunics, she glimmered sadly in sky-blue taffeta, in dusty turquoise crepe, a grown woman's dress made over, weighted by a big bow at the V of the neck and folding empty over Myra's narrow chest.

And I was glad she had not put it on. If someone asked her where she got it, and she told them, what would I say?

It was the day after this, or the week after, that Myra did not come to school. Often she was kept at home to help. But this time she did not come back. For a week, then two weeks, her desk was empty. Then we had a moving day at school and Myra's books were taken out of her desk and put on a shelf in the closet. Miss Darling said, "We'll find a seat when she comes back." And she stopped calling Myra's name when she took attendance.

Jimmy Sayla did not come to school either, having no one to take him to the bathroom.

In the fourth week or the fifth, that Myra had been away, Gladys Healey came to school and said, "Do you know what—Myra Sayla is sick in the hospital."

It was true. Gladys Healey had an aunt who was a nurse. Gladys put up her hand in the middle of Spelling and told Miss Darling. "I thought you might like to know," she said. "Oh yes," said Miss Darling. "I do know."

"What has she got?" we said to Gladys.

And Gladys said, "Akemia*, or something. And she has blood transfusions." She said to Miss Darling, "My aunt is a nurse."

So Miss Darling had the whole class write Myra a letter, in which everybody said, "Dear Myra, We are all writing you a letter. We hope you will soon be better and be back to school, Yours truly...." And Miss Darling said, "I've thought of something. Who would like to go up to the hospital and visit Myra on the twentieth of March, for a birthday party?"

I said, "Her birthday's in July."

"I know," said Miss Darling. "It's the twentieth of July. So this year she could have it on the twentieth of March, because she's sick."

"But her *birthday* is in July."

"Because she's sick," said Miss Darling, with a warning shrillness. "The cook at the hospital would make a cake and you could all give a little present, twenty-five cents or so. It would have to be between two and four, because that's visiting hours. And we couldn't all go, it'd be too many. So who wants to go and who wants to stay here and do supplementary reading?"

We all put up our hands. Miss Darling got out the spelling records and picked out the first fifteen, twelve girls and three boys. Then the three boys did not want to go so she picked out the next three girls. And I do not know when it was, but I think it was probably at this moment that the birthday party of Myra Sayla became fashionable.

Perhaps it was because Gladys Healey had an aunt who was a nurse, perhaps it was the excitement of sickness and hospitals, or simply the fact that Myra was so entirely, impressively set free of all the rules and conditions of our lives. We began to talk of her as if she were something we owned, and her party became a cause; with womanly heaviness we discussed it at recess, and decided that twenty-five cents was too low.

We all went up to the hospital on a sunny afternoon when the snow was melting, carrying our presents, and a nurse led us upstairs, single file, and down a hall past half-closed doors and dim conversations. She and Miss Darling kept saying, "Sh-sh," but we were going on tiptoe anyway; our hospital demeanor was perfect.

At this small country hospital there was no children's ward, and Myra was not really a child; they had put her in with two grey old women. A nurse was putting screens around them as we came in.

Myra was sitting up in bed, in a bulky stiff hospital gown. Her hair was down, the long braids falling over her shoulders and down the coverlet. But her face was the same, always the same.

She had been told something about the party, Miss Darling said, so the surprise would not upset her; but it seemed she had not believed, or had not understood what it was. She watched us as she used to watch in the school grounds when we played.

"Well, here we are!" said Miss Darling. "Here we are!"

And we said, "Happy birthday, Myra! Hello, Myra, happy birthday!" Myra said, "My birthday is in July." Her voice was lighter than ever, drifting, expressionless.

"Never mind when it is, really," said Miss Darling. "Pretend it's now! How old are you, Myra?"

"Eleven," Myra said. "In July."

Then we all took off our coats and emerged in our party dresses, and laid our presents, in their pale flowery wrappings on Myra's bed. Some of our mothers had made immense, complicated bows of fine satin ribbon, some of them had even taped on little bouquets of imitation roses and lilies of the valley. "Here Myra," we said, "here Myra, happy birthday." Myra did not look at us, but at the ribbons, pink and blue and speckled with silver, and the miniature bouquets; they pleased her, as the butterfly had done. An innocent look came into her face, a partial, private smile.

"Open them, Myra," said Miss Darling. "They're for you!"

Myra gathered the presents around her, fingering them, with this smile, and a cautious realization, an unexpected pride. She said, "Saturday I'm going to London to St. Joseph's Hospital."

"That's where my mother was at," somebody said. "We went and saw her. They've got all nuns there."

"My father's sister is a nun," said Myra calmly.

She began to unwrap the presents, with an air that not even Gladys could have bettered, folding the tissue paper and the ribbons, and drawing out books and puzzles and cutouts as if they were all prizes she had won. Miss Darling said that maybe she should say thank you, and the person's name with every gift she opened, to make sure she knew whom it was from, and so Myra said, "Thank you, Mary Louise, thank you, Carol," and when she came to mine she said, "Thank you, Helen." Everyone explained their presents to her and there was talking and excitement and a little gaiety, which Myra presided over, though she was not gay. A cake was brought in with *Happy Birthday Myra* written on it, pink on white, and eleven candles. Miss Darling lit the candles and we all sang Happy Birthday to You, and cried, "Make a wish, Myra, make a wish—" and Myra blew them out. Then we all had cake and strawberry ice cream.

At four o'clock a buzzer sounded and the nurse took out what was left of the cake, and the dirty dishes, and we put on our coats to go home. Everybody said, "Goodbye, Myra," and Myra sat in the bed watching us go, her back straight, not supported by any pillow, her hands resting on the gifts. But at the door I heard her call; she called, "Helen!" Only a couple of the others heard; Miss Darling did not hear, she had gone out ahead. I went back to the bed.

Myra said, "I got too many things. You take something."

"What?" I said. "It's for your birthday. You always get a lot at a birthday."

"Well you take something," Myra said. She picked up a leatherette case with a mirror in it, a comb and a nail file and a natural lipstick and a small handkerchief edged with gold thread. I had noticed it before. "You take that," she said.

"Don't you want it?"

"You take it." She put it into my hand. Our fingers touched again.

"When I come back from London," Myra said, "you can come and play at my place after school."

"Okay," I said. Outside the hospital window there was a clear carrying sound of somebody playing in the street, maybe chasing with the last snowballs of the year. This sound made Myra, her triumph and her bounty, and most of all her future in which she had found this place for me, turn shadowy, turn dark. All the presents on the bed, the folded paper and ribbons, those guilt-tinged offerings, had passed into this shadow, they were no longer innocent objects to be touched, exchanged, accepted without danger. I didn't want to take the case now but I could not think how to get out of it, what lie to tell. I'll give it away, I thought,

I won't ever play with it. I would let my little brother pull it apart.

The nurse came back, carrying a glass of chocolate milk.

"What's the matter, didn't you hear the buzzer?"

So I was released, set free by the barriers which now closed about Myra, her unknown, exalted, ether-smelling hospital world, and by the treachery of my own heart. "Well thank you," I said. "Thank you for the thing. Goodbye."

Did Myra ever say goodbye? Not likely. She sat in her high bed, her delicate brown neck rising out of a hospital gown too big for her, her brown carved face immune to treachery, her offering perhaps already forgotten, prepared to be set apart for legendary uses, as she was even in the back porch at school.

* **akemia:** leukemia

Darkness Box

URSULA K. LE GUIN

O n soft sand by the sea's edge a little boy walked leaving no footprints. Gulls cried in the bright sunless sky, trout leaped from the saltless ocean. Far off on the horizon the sea serpent raised himself a moment in seven enormous arches and then, bellowing, sank. The child whistled but the sea serpent, busy hunting whales, did not surface again. The child walked on casting no shadow, leaving no tracks on the sand between the cliffs and the sea. Ahead of him rose a grassy headland on which stood a four-legged hut. As he climbed a path up the cliff the hut skipped about and rubbed its front legs together like a lawyer or a fly; but the hands of the clock inside, which said ten minutes of ten, never moved.

"What's that you've got there, Dicky?" asked his mother as she added parsley and a pinch of pepper to the rabbit stew simmering in an alembic*.

"A box, Mummy."

"Where did you find it?"

Mummy's familiar* leaped down from the onion-festooned rafters and, draping itself like a foxfur round her neck, said, "By the sea."

Dicky nodded. "That's right. The sea washed it up."

"And what's inside it?"

The familiar said nothing, but purred. The witch turned round to look into her son's round face. "What's in it?" she repeated.

"Darkness."

"Oh? Let's see."

As she bent down to look the familiar, still purring, shut its eyes. Holding the box against his chest, the little boy very carefully lifted the lid a scant inch.

"So it is," said his mother. "Now put it away, don't let it get knocked about. I wonder where the key got to. Run wash your hands now. Table, lay!" And while the child worked the heavy pump-handle in the yard and splashed his face and hands, the hut resounded with the clatter of plates and forks materializing.

After the meal, while his mother was having her morning nap, Dicky took down the water-bleached, sand-encrusted box from his treasure shelf and set out with it across the dunes, away from the sea. Close at his heels the black familiar followed him, trotting patiently over the sand through the coarse grass, the only shadow he had.

At the summit of the pass Prince Rikard turned in the saddle to look back over the plumes and pennants of his army, over the long falling road, to the towered walls of his father's city. Under the sunless sky it shimmered there on the plain, fragile and shadowless as a pearl. Seeing it so he knew it could never be taken, and his heart sang with pride. He gave his captains the signal for quick march and set spurs to his horse. It reared and broke into a gallop, while his gryphon* swooped and screamed overhead. She teased the white horse, diving straight down at it clashing her beak, swerving aside just in time; the horse, bridleless, would snap furiously at her snaky tail or rear to strike out with silver hoofs. The gryphon would cackle and roar, circle back over the dunes and with a screech and swoop play the trick all over. Afraid she might wear herself out before the battle, Rikard finally leashed her, after which she flew along steadily, purring and chirping, by his side.

The sea lay before him; somewhere beneath the cliffs the enemy force his brother led was hidden. The road wound down growing sandier, the sea appearing to right or left always nearer. Abruptly the road fell away; the white horse leaped the ten-foot drop and galloped out over the beach. As he came out from beneath the dunes Rikard saw a long line of men strung out on the sand, and behind them three black-prowed ships. His own men were scrambling down the drop, swarming over the dunes, blue flags snapping in the sea wind, voices faint against the sound of the sea. Without warning or parley the two forces met, sword to sword and man to man. With a great shrilling scream the gryphon soared up, jerking the leash from Rikard's hand, then dropped like a falcon, beak and claws extended, down on a tall man in grey, the enemy leader. But the tall man's sword was drawn. As the iron beak snapped on his shoulder, trying to get the throat, the iron sword jabbed out and up, slashing the gryphon's belly. She doubled up in air and fell, knocking the man down with the sweep of her great wing, screaming, blackening the sand with blood. The tall man staggered up and slashed off her head and wings, turning half blinded with sand and blood only when Rikard was almost on him. Without a word he turned, lifting his steaming sword to parry Rikard's blow. He tried to strike at the horse's legs, but got no chance, for the beast would back and rear and run at him, Rikard's sword slashing down from above. The tall man's arms began to grow heavy, his breath came in gasps. Rikard gave no quarter*. Once more the tall man raised his sward, lunged, and took the whizzing slash of his brother's sword straight across his uplifted face. He fell without a word. Brown sand fell over his body in a little shower from the white stallion's hoofs as Rikard spurred back to the thick of the fight.

The attackers fought on doggedly, always fewer of them, and those few being pushed back step by step towards the sea. When only a knot of twenty or so remained they broke, sprinting desperately for the ships, pushing them off chest-deep in the breakers, clambering aboard. Rikard shouted to his men. They came to him across the sand, picking their way among hacked corpses. The badly wounded tried to crawl to him on hands and knees. All that could walk gathered in ranks in a hollow behind the dune on which Rikard stood. Behind him, out on deep water, the three black ships lay motionless, balanced on their oars.

Rikard sat down, alone on the dune-top among the rank grass. He bowed his head and put his hands over his face. Near him the white horse stood still as a horse of stone. Below him his men stood silent. Behind him on the beach the tall man, his face obliterated in blood, lay near the body of the gryphon, and the other dead lay staring at the sky where no sun shone.

A little gust of wind blew by. Rikard raised his face, which though young was very grim. He signalled his captains, swung up into the saddle, and set off round the dunes and back towards the city at a trot, not waiting to see the black ships steer in to shore where their soldiers could board them, or his own army fill up its ranks and come marching behind him. When the gryphon swooped screaming overhead he raised his arm, grinning at the great creature as she tried to perch on his gloved wrist, flapping her wings and screeching like a tomcat. "You no-good gryphon," he said, "you hen, go home to your chicken coop!" Insulted, the monster yawped and sailed off eastward towards the city. Behind him his army wound upward through the hills, leaving no track. Behind them the brown sand lay smooth as silk, stainless. The black ships, sails set, already stood out well to sea. In the prow of the first stood a tall, grim-faced man in grey.

Taking an easier road homeward, Rikard passed not far from the four-legged hut on the headland. The witch stood in the doorway, hailing him. He galloped over, and, drawing rein right at the gate of the little yard, he looked at the young witch. She was bright and dark as coals, her black hair whipped in the sea wind. She looked at him, white-armored on a white horse.

"Prince," she said, "you'll go to battle once too often."

He laughed. "What should I do—let my brother lay siege to the city?"

"Yes, let him. No man can take the city."

"I know. But my father the king exiled him, he must not set foot even on our shore. I'm my father's soldier, I fight as he commands."

The witch looked out to sea, then back to the young man. Her dark face sharpened, nose and chin peaking crone-like, eyes flashing. "Serve and be served," she said, "rule and be ruled. Your brother chose neither to serve nor rule.... Listen, prince, take care." Her face warmed again to beauty. "The sea brings presents this morning, the wind blows, the crystals break. Take care."

Gravely he bowed his thanks, then wheeled his horse and was gone, white as a gull over the long curve of the dunes.

The witch went back into the hut, glancing about its one room to see that everything was in place: bats, onions, cauldrons, carpets, broom, toad-stones, crystal balls (cracked through), the thin crescent moon hung up on the chimney, the Books, the familiar— She looked again, then hurried out and called "Dicky!"

The wind from the west was cold now, bending the coarse grass down.

"Dicky!... Kitty, kitty kitty!"

The wind caught the voice from her lips, tore it into bits and blew it away.

She snapped her fingers. The broom came zooming out the door, horizontal and about two feet off the ground, while the hut shivered and hopped about in excitement. "Shut up!" the witch snapped, and the door obediently slammed. Mounting the broom she took off in a long gliding swoop southwards down the beach, now and then crying out, "Dicky!... Here, kitty, kitty, kitty!"

The young prince, rejoining his men, had dismounted to walk with them. As they reached the pass and saw the city below them on the plain, he felt a tug at his cloak.

"Prince—"

A little boy, so little he was still fat and round-cheeked, stood with a scared look, holding up a battered, sandy box. Beside him a black cat sat smiling broadly. "The sea brought this—it's for the prince of the land, I know it is—please take it!"

"What's in it?"

"Darkness, sir."

Rikard took the box and after a slight hesitation opened it a little, just a crack. "It's painted black inside," he said with a hard grin.

"No, prince, truly it's not. Open it wider!"

Cautiously Rikard lifted the lid higher, an inch or two, and peered in. Then he shut it quickly, even as the child said, "Don't let the wind blow it out, prince!"

"I shall take this to the king."

"But it's for you, sir—"

"All seagifts are the king's. But thank you for it, boy." They looked at each other for a moment, the little round boy and the hard splendid youth; then Rikard turned and strode on, while Dicky wandered back down the hills, silent and disconsolate. He heard his mother's voice from far away to the south, and tried to answer; but the wind blew his call landwards, and the familiar had disappeared.

The bronze gates of the city swung open as the troop approached. Watchdogs bayed, guards stood rigid, the people of the city bowed down as Rikard on his horse clattered at full gallop up the marble streets to the palace. Entering, he glanced up at the great bronze clock on the bell-tower, the highest of the nine white towers of the palace. The moveless hands said ten minutes of ten.

In the Hall of Audience his father awaited him: a fierce grey-haired man crowned with iron, his hands clenched on the heads of iron chimaeras* that formed the arms of the throne. Rikard knelt and with bowed head, never looking up, reported the success of his foray. "The Exile was killed, with the greater part of his men; the rest fled in their ships."

A voice answered like an iron door moving on unused hinges: "Well done, prince."

"I bring you a seagift, Lord." Still with head bowed, Rikard held up the wooden box.

A low snarl came from the throat of one of the carven monsters of the throne.

"That is mine," said the old king so harshly that Rikard glanced up for a second, seeing the teeth of the chimaeras bared and the king's eyes glittering.

"Therefore I bring it to you, Lord."

"That is mine—I gave it to the sea, I myself! And the sea spits back my gift." A long silence, then the king spoke more softly. "Well, keep it, prince. The sea doesn't want it, nor do I. It's in your hands. Keep it—locked. Keep it locked, prince!"

Rikard, on his knees, bowed lower in thanks and consent, then rose and backed down the long hall, never looking up. As he came out into the glittering anteroom, officers and noblemen gathered round him, ready as usual to ask about the battle, laugh, drink, and chatter. He passed among them without a word or glance and went to his own quarters, alone, carrying the box carefully in both hands.

His bright, shadowless, windowless room was decorated on every wall with patterns of gold inset with topazes, opals, crystals, and, most vivid of all jewels, candle flames moveless on golden sconces. He set the box down on a glass table, threw off his cloak, unbuckled his swordbelt, and sat down sighing. The gryphon loped in from his bedroom, talons rasping on the mosaic floor, stuck her great head onto his knees and waited for him to scratch her feathery mane. There was also a cat prowling around the room, a sleek black one; Rikard took no notice. The palace was full of animals, cats, hounds, apes, squirrels, young hippogriffs*, white mice, tigers. Every lady had her unicorn, every courtier had a dozen pets. The prince had only one, the gryphon which always fought for him, his one unquestioning friend. He scratched the gryphon's mane, often glancing down to meet the loving golden gaze of her round eyes, now and then glancing too at the box on the table. There was no key to lock it.

Music played softly in a distant room, a ceaseless interweaving of notes like the sound of a fountain.

He turned to look at the clock on the mantle, an ornate square of gold and blue enamel. It was ten minutes of ten: time to rise and buckle on his sword, call up his men, and go to battle. The Exile was returning, determined to take the city and reclaim his right to the throne, his inheritance. His black ships must be driven back to sea. The brothers must fight, and one must die, and the city be saved. Rikard rose, and at once the gryphon jumped up lashing her tail, eager for the fight. "All right, come along!" Rikard told her, but his voice was cold. He took up his sword in the pearl-encrusted sheath and buckled it on, and the gryphon whined with excitement and rubbed her beak on his hand. He did not respond. He was tired and sad, he longed for something—for what? To hear music that ceased, to speak to his brother once before they fought...he did not know. Heir and defender, he must obey. He set the silver helmet on his head and turned to pick up his cloak, flung over a chair. The pearly sheath slung from his belt clattered against something behind him; he turned and saw the box, lying on the floor, open. As he stood looking at it with the same cold, absent look, a little blackness like smoke gathered about it on the floor. He stooped and picked it up, and darkness ran out over his hands.

The gryphon backed away, whining.

Tall and white-armored, fair-haired, silver-capped in the glittering shadowless room, Rikard stood holding the open box, watching the thick dusk that dripped slowly from it. All around his body now, below his hands, was twilight. He stood still. Then slowly he raised the box up, clear up over his head, and turned it upside down.

Darkness flowed over his face. He looked about him, for the distant music had stopped and things were very silent. Candles burned, dots of light picking out flecks of gold and flashes of violet from walls and ceiling. But all the corners were dark, behind each chair lay darkness, and as Rikard turned his head his shadow leapt along the wall. He moved then, quickly, dropping the box, for in one of the black corners he had glimpsed the reddish glow of two great eyes. —The gryphon, of course. He held out his hand and spoke to her. She did not move, but gave a queer metallic cry.

"Come on! Are you afraid of the dark?" he said, and then all at once was afraid himself. He drew his sword. Nothing moved. He took a step backward towards the door; and the monster jumped. He saw the black wings spread across the ceiling, the iron beak, the talons; her bulk was on him before he could stab upwards. He wrestled, the great beak snapping at his throat and the talons tearing at his arms and chest, till he got his sword-arm free and could slash down, pull away and slash again. The second blow half severed the gryphon's neck. She dropped off, lay writhing in the shadows among splinters of glass, then lay still.

Rikard's sword dropped clattering on the floor. His hands were sticky with his own blood, and he could hardly see; the beating of the gryphon's wings had blown out or knocked over every candle but one. He groped his way to a chair and sat down. After a minute, though he still gasped for breath, he did as he had done on the dune-top after battle: bowed his head and hid his face in his hands. It was completely silent. The one candle flickered in its sconce, mirrored feebly in a cluster of topazes on the wall behind it. Rikard raised his head.

The gryphon lay still. Its blood had spread out in a pool, black as the first spilt darkness from the box. Its iron beak was open, its eyes open, like two red stones.

"It's dead," said a small soft voice, as the witch's cat came picking its way delicately among the fragments of the smashed table. "Once and for all. Listen, prince!" The cat sat down curling its tail neatly round its paw. Rickard stood motionless, blank-faced, till a sudden sound made him start: a little ting! nearby. Then from the tower overhead a huge dull bell-stroke reverberted in the stone of the floor, in his ears, in his blood. The clocks were striking ten.

There was a pounding at his door, and shouts echoed down the palace corridors mixed with the last booming strokes of the bell, screams of scared animals, calls, commands.

"You'll be late for the battle, prince," said the cat.

Rikard groped among blood and shadow for his sword, sheathed it, flung on his cloak and went to the door.

"There'll be an afternoon today," the cat said, "and a twilight, and night will fall. At nightfall one of you will come home to the city, you or your brother. But only one of you, prince."

Rikard stood still a moment. "Is the sun shining now, outside?"

"Yes, it is—now."

"Well, then, it's worth it," the young man said, and opened the door and strode on out into the hubbub and panic of the sunlit halls, his shadow falling black behind him.

* **alembic:** cup or vessel used to hold potions or for distilling
* **familiar:** animal or spirit attending on and obeying a witch; usually, as here, a cat
* **gryphon:** mythological beast, part eagle and part lion
* **gave no quarter:** refused to back away; did not give an inch
* **chimaera:** mythological beast, part lion, part goat and part serpent
* **hippogriff:** mythological beast, part eagle and part horse

The Magic Chalk

ABE KOBO

Next door to the toilet of an apartment building on the edge of the city, in a room soggy with roof leaks and cooking vapors, lived a poor artist named Argon.

The small room, nine feet square, appeared to be larger than it was because it contained nothing but a single chair set against the wall. His desk, shelves, paint box, even his easel had been sold for bread. Now only the chair and Argon were left. But how long would these two remain?

Dinnertime drew near. "How sensitive my nose has become!" Argon thought. He was able to distinguish the colors and proximity of the complex aromas entering his room. Frying pork at the butcher's along the streetcar line: yellow ocher. A southerly wind drifting by the front of the fruit stand: emerald green. Wafting from the bakery: stimulating chrome yellow. And the fish the housewife below was broiling, probably mackerel: sad cerulean blue.

The fact is, Argon hadn't eaten anything all day. With a pale face, a wrinkled brow, an Adam's apple that rose and fell, a hunched back, a sunken abdomen, and trembling knees, Argon thrust both hands into his pockets and yawned three times in succession.

His fingers found a stick in his pocket.

"Hey, what's this? Red chalk. Don't remember it being there."

Playing with the chalk between his fingers, he produced another large yawn.

"Aah, I need something to eat."

Without realizing it, Argon began scribbling on the wall with the chalk. First, an apple. One that looked big enough to be a meal in itself. He drew a paring knife beside it so that he could eat it right away. Next, swallowing hard as baking smells curled through the hallway and window to permeate his room, he drew bread. Jam-filled bread the size of a baseball glove. Butter-filled rolls. A loaf as large as a person's head. He envisioned glossy browned spots on the bread. Delicious-looking cracks, dough bursting through the surface, the intoxicating aroma of yeast. Beside the bread, then, a stick of butter as large as a brick. He thought of drawing some coffee. Freshly brewed, steaming coffee. In a large, juglike cup. On a saucer, three matchbox-size sugar cubes.

"Damn it!" He ground his teeth and buried his face in his hands. "I've got to eat!"

Gradually his consciousness sank into darkness. Beyond the windowpane was a bread and pastry jungle, a mountain of canned goods, a sea of milk, a beach of sugar, a beef and cheese orchard—he scampered about until, fatigued, he fell asleep.

A heavy thud on the floor and the sound of smashing crockery woke him up. The sun had already set. Pitch black. Bewildered, he glanced toward the noise and gasped. A broken cup. The spilled liquid, still steaming, was definitely coffee, and near it were the apple, bread, butter, sugar, spoon, knife, and (luckily unbroken) the saucer. The pictures he had chalked on the wall had vanished.

"How could it...?"

Suddenly every vein in his body was wide awake and pounding. Argon stealthily crept closer.

"No, no, it can't be. But look, it's real. Nothing fake about the smothering aroma of this coffee. And here, the bread is smooth to the touch. Be bold, taste it. Argon, don't you believe it's real even now? Yes, it's real. I believe it. But frightening. To believe it is frightening. And yet, it's real. It's edible!"

The apple tasted like an apple (a "snow" apple). The bread tasted like bread (American flour). The butter tasted like butter (same contents as the label on the wrapper—not margarine). The sugar tasted like sugar (sweet). Ah, they all tasted like the real thing. The knife gleamed, reflecting his face.

By the time he came to his senses, Argon had somehow finished eating and heaved a sigh of relief. But when he recalled why he had sighed like this, he immediately became confused again. He took the chalk in his fingers and stared at it intently. No matter how much he scrutinized it, he couldn't understand what he didn't understand. He decided to make sure by trying it once more. If he succeeded a second time, then he would have to concede that it had actually happened. He thought he would try to draw something different, but in his haste just drew another familiar-looking apple. As soon as he finished drawing, it fell easily from the wall. So this is real after all. A repeatable fact.

Joy suddenly turned his body rigid. The tips of his nerves broke through his skin and stretched out toward the universe, rustling like fallen leaves. Then, abruptly, the tension eased, and, sitting down on the floor, he burst out laughing like a panting goldfish.

"The laws of the universe have changed. My fate has changed, misfortune has taken its leave. Ah, the age of fulfillment, a world of desires realized... God, I'm sleepy. Well, then, I'll draw a bed. This chalk has become as precious as life itself, but a bed is something you always need after eating your fill, and it never really wears out, so no need to be miserly about it. Ah, for the first time in my life I'll sleep like a lamb."

One eye soon fell asleep, but the other lay awake. After today's contentment he was uneasy about what tomorrow might bring. However, the other eye, too, finally closed in sleep. With eyes working out of sync he dreamed mottled dreams throughout the night.

Well, this worrisome tomorrow dawned in the following manner.

He dreamed that he was being chased by a ferocious beast and fell off a bridge. He had fallen off the bed... No. When he awoke, there was no bed anywhere. As usual, there was nothing but that one chair. Then what had happened last night? Argon timidly looked around at the wall, tilting his head.

There, in red chalk, were drawings of a cup (it was broken!), a spoon, a knife, apple peel, and a butter wrapper. Below these was a bed—a picture of the bed off which he was supposed to have fallen.

Among all of last night's drawings, only those he could not eat had once again become pictures and returned to the wall. Suddenly he felt pain in his hip and shoulder. Pain in precisely the place he should feel it if he had indeed fallen out of bed. He gingerly touched the sketch of the bed where the sheets had been rumpled by sleep and felt a slight warmth, clearly distinguishable from the coldness of the rest of the drawing.

He brushed his finger along the blade of the knife picture. It was certainly nothing more than chalk; there was no resistance, and it disappeared leaving only a smear. As a test he decided to draw a new apple. It neither turned into a real apple and fell nor even peeled off like a piece of unglued paper, but rather vanished beneath his chafed palm into the surface of the wall.

His happiness had been merely a single night's dream. It was all over, back to what it was before anything had happened. Or was it really? No, his misery had returned fivefold. His hunger pangs attacked him fivefold. It seemed that all he had eaten had been restored in his stomach to the original substances of wall and chalk powder.

When he had gulped from his cupped hands a pint or so of water from the communal sink, he set out toward the lonely city, still enveloped in the mist of early dawn. Leaning over an open drain that ran from the kitchen of a restaurant about a hundred yards ahead, he thrust his hands into the viscous, tarlike sewage and pulled something out. It was a basket made of wire netting. He washed it in a small brook nearby. What was left in it seemed edible, and he was particulary heartened that half of it looked like rice. An old man in his apartment building had told him recently that by placing the basket in the drain one could obtain enough food for a meal a day. Just about a month ago the man had found the means to afford bean curd lees, so he had ceded the restaurant drain to the artist.

Recalling last night's feast, this was indeed muddy, unsavory fare. But it wasn't magic. What actually helped fill his stomach was precious and so could not be rejected. Even if its nastiness made him aware of every swallow, he must eat it. This was the real thing.

Just before noon he entered the city and dropped in on a friend who was employed at a bank. The friend smiled wryly and asked, "My turn today?"

Stiff and expressionless, Argon nodded. As always, he received half of his friend's lunch, bowed deeply and left.

For the rest of the day, Argon thought.

He held the chalk lightly in his hand, leaned back in the chair, and as he sat absorbed in his daydreams about magic, anticipation began to crystallize around that urgent longing. Finally, evening once again drew near. His hope that at sunset the magic might take effect had changed into near confidence.

Somewhere a noisy radio announced that it was five o'clock. He stood up and on the wall drew bread and butter, a can of sardines, and coffee, not forgetting to add a table underneath so as to prevent anything from falling and breaking as had occurred the previous night. Then he waited.

Before long darkness began to crawl quietly up the wall from the corners of the room. In order to verify the course of the magic, he turned on the light. He had already confirmed last night that electric light did it no harm.

The sun had set. The drawings on the wall began to fade, as if his vision had blurred. It seemed as if a mist was caught between the wall and his eyes. The pictures grew increasingly faint, and the mist grew dense. And soon, just as he had anticipated, the mist had settled into solid shapes—success! The contents of the pictures suddenly appeared as real objects.

The steamy coffee was tempting, the bread freshly baked and still warm.

"Oh! Forgot a can opener."

He held his left hand underneath to catch it before it fell, and, as he drew, the outlines took on material form. His drawing had literally come to life.

All of a sudden, he stumbled over something. Last night's bed "existed" again. Moreover, the knife handle (he had erased the blade with his finger), the butter wrapper, and the broken cup lay fallen on the floor.

After filling his empty stomach, Argon lay down on the bed.

"Well, what shall it be next? It's clear now that the magic doesn't work in daylight. Tomorrow I'll have to suffer all over again. There must be a simple way out of this. Ah, yes! a brilliant plan—I'll cover up the window and shut myself in darkness."

He would need some money to carry out the project. To

keep out the sun required some objects that would not lose their substance when exposed to sunlight. But drawing money is a bit difficult. He racked his brains, then drew a purse full of money... The idea was a success, for when he opened up the purse he found more than enough bills stuffed inside.

This money, like the counterfeit coins that badgers made from tree leaves in the fairy tale*, would disappear in the light of day, but it would leave no trace behind, and that was a great relief. He was cautious nonetheless and deliberately proceeded toward a distant town. Two heavy blankets, five sheets of black woolen cloth, a piece of felt, a box of nails, and four pieces of squared lumber. In addition, one volume of a cookbook collection that caught his eye in a second-hand bookstore along the way. With the remaining money he bought a cup of coffee, not in the least superior to the coffee he had drawn on the wall. He was (why?) proud of himself. Lastly, he bought a newspaper.

He nailed the door shut, then attached two layers of cloth and a blanket. With the rest of the material, he covered the window, and he blocked the edges with the wood. A feeling of security, and at the same time a sense of being attacked by eternity, weighed upon him. Argon's mind grew distant, and, lying down on the bed, he soon fell asleep.

Sleep neither diminished nor neutralized his happiness in the slightest. When he awoke, the steel springs throughout his body were coiled and ready to leap, full of life. A new day, a new time...tomorrow wrapped in a mist of glittering gold dust, and the day after tomorrow, and more and more overflowing armfuls of tomorrows were waiting expectantly. Argon smiled, overcome with joy. Now, at this very moment, everything, without any hindrance whatsoever, was waiting eagerly among myriad possibilities to be created by his own hand. It was a brilliant moment. But what, in the depths of his heart, was this faintly aching sorrow? It might have been the sorrow that God had felt just before Creation. Beside the muscles of his smile, smaller muscles twitched slightly.

Argon drew a large wall clock. With a trembling hand he set the clock precisely at twelve, determining at that moment the start of a new destiny.

He thought the room was a bit stuffy, so he drew a window on the wall facing the hallway. Hm, what's wrong? The window didn't materialize. Perplexed for a moment, he then realized that the window could not acquire any substance because it did not have an outside; it was not equipped with all the conditions necessary to make it a window.

"Well, then, shall I draw an outside? What kind of view would be nice? Shall it be the Alps or the Bay of Naples? A quiet pastoral scene wouldn't be bad. Then again, a primeval Siberian forest might be interesting." All the beautiful landscapes he had seen on postcards and in travel guides flickered before him. But he had to choose one from among them all, and he couldn't make up his mind. "Well, let's attend to pleasure first," he decided. He drew some whiskey and cheese and, as he nibbled, slowly thought about it.

The more he thought, the less he understood.

"This isn't going to be easy. It could involve work on a larger scale than anything I—or anyone—has ever tried to design. In fact, now that I think about it, it wouldn't do simply to draw a few streams and orchards, mountains and seas, and other things pleasing to the eye. Suppose I drew a mountain; it would no longer be just a mountain. What would be beyond it? A city? A sea? A desert? What kind of people would be living there? What kind of animals? Unconsciously I would be deciding those things. No, making this window a window is serious business. It involves the creation of a world. Defining a world with just a few lines. Would it be right to leave that to chance? No, the scene outside can't be casually drawn. I must produce the kind of picture that no human hand has yet achieved."

Argon sank into deep contemplation.

The first week passed in discontent as he pondered a design for a world of infinitude. Canvases once again lined his room, and the smell of turpentine hung in the air. Dozens of rough sketches accumulated in a pile. The more he thought, however, the more extensive the problem became, until finally he felt it was all too much for him. He thought he might boldly leave it up to chance, but in that case his efforts to create a new world would come to nothing. And if he merely captured accurately the inevitability of partial reality, the contradictions inherent in that reality would pull him back into the past, perhaps trapping him again in starvation. Besides, the chalk had a limited lifespan. He had to capture the world.

The second week flew by in inebriation and gluttony.

The third week passed in a despair resembling insanity. Once again his canvases lay covered with dust, and the smell of oils had faded.

In the fourth week Argon finally made up his mind, a result of nearly total desperation. He just couldn't wait any longer. In order to evade the responsibility of creating with his own hand an outside for the window, he decided to take a great risk that would leave everything to chance.

"I'll draw a door on the wall. The outside will be decided by whatever is beyond the door. Even if it ends in failure, even if it turns out to be the same apartment scene as before, it'll be far better than being tormented by this responsibility. I don't care what happens, better to escape."

Argon put on a jacket for the first time in a long while. It was a ceremony in honor of the establishment of the world, so one couldn't say he was being extravagant. With a stiff hand he lowered the chalk of destiny. A picture of the door. He was breathing hard. No wonder. Wasn't the sight beyond the door the greatest mystery a man could contemplate? Perhaps death was awaiting him as his reward.

He grasped the knob. He took a step back and opened the door.

Dynamite pierced his eyes, exploding. After a while he opened them fearfully to an awesome wasteland glaring in the noonday sun. As far as he could see, with the exception of the horizon, there was not a single shadow. To the extent that he could peer into the dark sky, not a single cloud. A hot dry wind blew past, stirring up a dust storm.

"Aah... It's just as though the horizon line in one of my designs had become the landscape itself. Aah..."

The chalk hadn't resolved anything after all. He still had to create it all from the beginning. He had to fill this desolate land with mountains, water, clouds, trees, plants, birds, beasts, fish. He had to draw the world all over again. Discouraged, Argon collapsed onto the bed. One after another, tears fell unceasingly.

Something rustled in his pocket. It was the newspaper he had bought on that first day and forgotten about. The headline on the first page read, "Invasion Across Thirty-eighth Parallel!" On the second page, an even larger space devoted to a photograph of Miss Nippon*. Underneath, in small print, "Riot at N Ward Employment Security Office," and "Large-scale Dismissals at U Factory."

Argon stared at the half-naked Miss Nippon. What intense longing. What a body. Flesh of glass.

"This is what I forgot. Nothing else matters. It's time to begin everything from Adam and Eve. That's it—Eve! I'll draw Eve!"

Half an hour later Eve was standing before him, stark naked. Startled, she looked around her.

"Oh! Who are you? What's happened? Golly, I'm naked!"

"I am Adam. You are Eve." Argon blushed bashfully.

"I'm Eve, you say? Ah, no wonder I'm naked. But why are you wearing clothes? Adam, in Western dress—now that's weird."

Suddenly her tone changed.

"You're lying! I'm not Eve. I'm Miss Nippon."

"You're Eve. You really are Eve."

"You expect me to believe this is Adam—in those clothes—in a dump like this? Come on, give me back *my* clothes. What am I doing here anyway? I'm due to make a special modeling appearance at a photo contest."

"Oh, no. You don't understand. You're Eve, I mean it."

"Give me a break, will you? Okay, where's the apple? And I suppose this is the Garden of Eden? Ha, don't make me laugh. Now give me my clothes."

"Well, at least listen to what I have to say. Sit down over there. Then I'll explain everything. By the way, can I offer you something to eat?"

"Yes, go ahead. But hurry up and give me my clothes, okay? My body's valuable."

"What would you like? Choose anything you want from this cookbook."

"Oh, great! Really? The place is filthy, but you must be pretty well fixed. I've changed my mind. Maybe you really are Adam after all. What do you do for a living? Burglar?"

"No, I'm Adam. Also an artist, and a world planner."

"I don't understand."

"Neither do I. That's why I'm depressed."

Watching Argon draw the food with swift strokes as he spoke, Eve shouted, "Hey, great, that's great. This *is* Eden, isn't it? Wow. Yeah, okay, I'll be Eve. I don't mind being Eve. We're going to get rich—right?"

"Eve, please listen to me."

In a sad voice, Argon told her his whole story, adding finally, "So you see, with your cooperation we must design this world. Money's irrelevant. We have to start everything from scratch."

Miss Nippon was dumbfounded.

"Money's irrelevant, you say? I don't understand. I don't get it. I absolutely do not understand."

"If you're going to talk like that, well, why don't you open this door and take a look outside."

She glanced through the door Argon had left half open.

"My God! How awful!"

She slammed the door shut and glared at him.

"But how about *this* door," she said, pointing to his real, blanketed door. "Different, I'll bet."

"No, don't. That one's no good. It will just wipe out this world, the food, desk, bed, and even you. *You* are the new Eve. And we must become the father and mother of our world."

"Oh no. No babies. I'm all for birth control. I mean, they're such a bother. And besides, I won't disappear."

"You will disappear."

"I won't. I know myself best. I'm me. All this talk about disappearing—you're really weird."

"My dear Eve, you don't know. If we don't re-create the world, then sooner or later we're faced with starvation."

"What? Calling me 'dear' now, are you? You've got a nerve. And you say I'm going to starve. Don't be ridiculous. My body's valuable."

"No, your body's the same as my chalk. If we don't acquire a world of our own, your existence will just be a fiction. The same as nothing at all."

"Okay, that's enough of this junk. Come on, give me back my clothes. I'm leaving. No two ways about it, my being here is weird. I shouldn't be here. You're a magician or something. Well, hurry up. My manager's probably fed up with waiting. If you want me to drop in and be your Eve every now and then, I don't mind. As long as you use your chalk to give me what I want."

"Don't be a fool! You can't do that."

The abrupt, violent tone of Argon's voice startled her, and she looked into his face. They both stared at each other for a moment in silence. Whatever was in her thoughts, she then said calmly, "All right, I'll stay. But, in exchange, will you grant me one wish?"

"What is it? If you stay with me, I'll listen to anything you have to say."

"I want half of your chalk."

"That's unreasonable. After all, dear, you don't know how to draw. What good would it do you?"

"I do know how to draw. I may not look like it, but I used to be a designer. I insist on equal rights."

He tilted his head for an instant, then straightening up again, said decisively, "All right, I believe you."

He carefully broke the chalk in half and gave one piece to Eve. As soon as she received it, she turned to the wall and began drawing.

It was a pistol.

"Stop it! What are you going to do with that thing?"

"Death, I'm going to make death. We need some divisions. They're very important in making a world."

"No, that'll be the end. Stop it. It's the most unnecessary thing of all."

But it was too late. Eve was clutching a small pistol in her hand. She raised it and aimed directly at his chest.

"Move and I'll shoot. Hands up. You're stupid, Adam. Don't you know that a promise is the beginning of a lie? It's you who made me lie."

"What? *Now* what are you drawing?"

"A hammer. To smash the door down."

"You can't!"

"Move and I'll shoot!"

The moment he leaped the pistol rang out. Argon held his chest as his knees buckled and he collapsed to the floor. Oddly, there was no blood.

"Stupid Adam."

Eve laughed. Then, raising the hammer, she struck the door. The light streamed in. It wasn't very bright, but it was real. Light from the sun. Eve was suddenly absorbed, like mist. The desk, the bed, the French meal, all disappeared. All but Argon, the cookbook which had landed on the floor, and the chair were transformed back into pictures on the wall.

Argon stood up unsteadily. His chest wound had healed. But something stronger than death was summoning him, compelling him—the wall. The wall was calling him. His body, which had eaten drawings from the wall continuously for four weeks, had been almost entirely transformed by them. Resistance was impossible now. Argon staggered toward the wall and was drawn in on top of Eve.

The sound of the gunshot and the door being smashed

were heard by others in the building. By the time they ran in, Argon had been completely absorbed into the wall and had become a picture. The people saw nothing but the chair, the cookbook, the scribblings on the wall. Staring at Argon lying on top of Eve, someone remarked, "Starved for a woman, wasn't he."

"Doesn't it look just like him, though?" said another.

"What was he doing, destroying the door like that? And look at this, the wall's covered with scribbles. Huh. He won't get away with it. Where in the world did he disappear to? Calls himself a painter!"

The man grumbling to himself was the apartment manager.

After everyone left, there came a murmuring from the wall.

"It isn't chalk that will remake the world..."

A single drop welled out of the wall. It fell from just below the eye of the pictorial Argon.

* **the counterfeit coins that badgers made from tree leaves in the fairy tale:** there are several versions of this tale; see, for instance, "The Good Fortune Kettle" in *Told in Japan* by Virginia Haviland

* **Nippon:** the Japanese name for Japan

Grandmother

FRANCES ITANI

The family sits in rows all the way to the back of the funeral parlour, spilling over into two side-rooms, but the minister places himself behind the coffin and at an angle that permits him to face my grandmother directly, almost to the exclusion of daughters and sons, grandchildren and great-grandchildren. For my grandmother will lip-read this service just as she has lip-read every human communication that has come her way from the mouths of others throughout her eighty-five years.

She is small in stature but there is no suggestion of frailty in her bearing; indeed, the words frail or weak have nothing whatever to do with this woman. To a stranger's eye—even to many family friends now present—she is composed as she always is, her soft-lined cheeks touched lightly with rouge, her hair in a never-severe figure-eight at the back of her neck. But her thirteen sons and daughters, some of her fifty-eight grandchildren and even a few of her great-grandchildren will know, by the fact that one foot is crossed over the other and now moves to a private rhythm of its own, the extent of her inner agitation. For sometimes it is the only measure we have of her.

"Look at Ma's foot," her sons and daughters have always said when they have been together for any sort of family gathering. "Look at Ma's foot going." And sometimes, "We'd better look out." For it has been for them not only a yardstick of joy or of sorrow, but even one of anger—though of the latter I myself have never seen a sign. She reaches a hand up now to push a loose strand of hair into place and I am reminded that it has been almost two years since I have seen her with her hair down. It was once reddish-brown, long and flowing, and even now, despite the grey and white at the top and sides, one can see touches of red in the figure-eight. The last time I visited her, I brought a friend with me, from the city. As we sat in her bedroom one evening going through cigar boxes of old photographs, my grandmother suddenly appeared in the doorway wearing a dressing gown and carrying a long wooden tray made by my grandfather and painted by her. The tray was heavy with an enormous pot of tea under a quilted tea cosy and biscuits and cake, and after my grandmother had set this down on a table she stood at the end of the bed and began to turn slowly, like a small grand queen. With her back to us she reached up and loosened the long hairpins and fanned the hair out softly over her back. It had never been cut and reached down past her thighs. She turned, faced us with hairpins between her teeth, and swiftly gathered the hair, looping it several times over her wrist and arm before pinning it up again. She had done this, I knew, because she liked and approved of my friend.

My grandmother looks straight ahead, watching the minister's lips; it is evident that he is trying to form his words the way he has seen the family speak. Indeed, I cannot even imagine how we must appear to an outsider when more than a few members of this large family are in one room at the same time. We are perhaps louder than most families, partly because we may have to shout to be heard when there is always so much competition in numbers, and partly because of my grandmother. We all *know* that shouting will not help her hearing—not a bit. The scar tissue in her ears is so thick and layered that even when hearing-aids were invented, modified, improved, they were of no use to her. When we do speak to her, we do not shout at all; we more or less speak in a loud hoarse whisper so that others present in the same room will be able to follow the conversation. For most of the conversation will be directed at or to my grandmother. Something to do with her deaf-mute state has made her eyes quick and alert. Her thirteen children will testify that it has never been easy to fool her. Yet they did succeed, over the years, in building a childish network of communications with one another: quick half-turns over the shoulder, shouts from other rooms (when grandfather was not in the house). When we speak to her, we carefully animate and enlarge every word on our lips so that she can easily discern one word from another. Her children are best at this, of course. The others, one or more generations removed, practise in imitation. As she can feel vibrations, there is also directed at her—at any given time—a good deal of table-banging, skirt-pulling, shoulder-tapping and foot-stomping. When my grandmother feels the floor vibrate or the table shudder, she looks instantly to the source and reads on our lips the message we have for her. But the family is so accustomed to banging and stomping, shouting and enunciating, that we carry on in the same way, even when she is not with us. We slip into imitations of "grandmother-present-speech" when we discuss things she has said or when we are telling a story in which she has had a part.

Though outsiders cannot readily understand my grandmother's speech, the family, of course, can. It is a wonder to see how the smallest and youngest of the great-grandchildren stands before her, tugging at her skirt, exaggerating his lip movements. Satisfied with her response, he turns away, giving his arms a little flap against his sides, immensely pleased with himself—as if rejoicing after having been given a wonderful and rare gift. In this small child I see all of us, remembering the pleasure and satisfaction: the realization that we have had our private communication with Grandmother.

It is difficult to think of any one part of this family without thinking of all parts: the brown-and-white photographs of the sons and daughters of the farm, propped on adult knees, wearing white sweet-pea-looking gowns and having sad dark eyes; the house of smooth worn curves, the stone kitchen being added as an afterthought or perhaps as more babies were born; the huge barn my grandfather built; the stories. For this family is a family of storytellers, and through the years there have been many stories to tell. When a person begins to tell a story, it is one of the few times others temporarily fall into silence in the background. For a story is an evocation of the past, which belongs to all of us, and there is not one of us who does not in at least some small but undefined way, respect that which has been handed on to us by this old woman. She sits now, watching the minister's every facial movement as he speaks of the man who has been her companion and partner for more than sixty years. There is a question in the background—lying poised and unasked and ready to spring: "What will Grandmother do?" For we have sought, in Grandmother and Grandfather, a permanency that has already begun to crumble. My grandmother has never been left alone. It is unthinkable, even to her, that she would remain at the farm by herself. My grandfather has been as much her shield from the world as we, children and children's children, have been her exposure.

From the time that I was very young I held some sort of awareness of the excitement and wonderment of belonging to such a family. My own father and mother lived in another province and it was only during the summers that I and my brothers and sisters could and did return with my mother and sometimes with both parents to the farm. That such a place could exist that could contain the complexities of the lives of so many people at the same time, was enough to cause me to stand timidly on the two wooden steps that divided the stone kitchen from the dining room, staring, collecting sounds, sights, smells and sensations that would remain with me during all of my adult years in other parts of the world.

I knew that my own mother, eldest of thirteen, had been born prematurely in my grandmother's bedroom up over the kitchen, while the wedding party of my grandfather's brother was in progress in the rooms below. Grandmother gave silent birth while the fiddles played; cut off from the celebrations by kerosene shadows falling against the wall behind her, by her handicap and her fear. And my mother, a seven-month arrival over whom the sobered wedding guests clucked sadly as she was wrapped in cotton batting and placed like a fragile egg in a shoebox in the oven, survived to perch for the camera proudly and robustly, like a fattened white bird on my grandfather's shoulder, six months later.

My own birth was as encompassed by fear as the birth of my mother nineteen years before, she having returned to the farm to help with the pickling and preserving in the late summer and learning quickly, when there was no time to get her mother to hospital, that she was to assist at the birth of her youngest brother, my uncle, born two days before me. He was delivered by old Dr. Church, who had helped with each of the other twelve, ten at the farm and two in hospital (times were changing). Two days later Dr. Church delivered me and later, my brothers and sisters, my mother returning by train at the end of each gestation to the family doctor's trust and care.

It was not until I became a woman myself that my mother told me how all of her younger sisters and brothers were shooed from the farmhouse to wait outside while my grandmother bore her final son. In the narrow upstairs room Dr. Church looked steadily across the bed to my mother and said, "You can do it, Nessa," knowing she was nine months pregnant herself. My mother clasped the mask* to her own mother's face, and did all of the things that had to be done for Dr. Church as he struggled with a stubbornly placed breech and kept my haemorrhaging grandmother and the newborn alive.

I think of a group of us, timeless, sitting around a kitchen table, anywhere. My grandmother's feet are crossed, one over the other. She is waiting for someone to explain a joke that has caused us to burst into laughter; she searches our faces while we go through it carefully line by line. She leans back; her foot jigs impatiently; her eyes flicker and her head nods and she says, "I see, I see," which sounds like a mixture of a song and a sigh and which, whenever I think of her like this, causes me to have an enormous feeling of love for her, no matter how far away I may be. Her face and her shoulders seem to fold into laughter as she, then understanding, joins with the others until tears pour from our eyes and hers; and those who wear glasses must remove them to wipe their eyes because all of us in the family have inherited tears that weep and overflow with the act of laughter.

I think of my grandmother watching the door today as my husband and I enter the funeral parlour—we having had the longest journey and arriving last—and she, as she kisses us, saying, "Everyone is here now." Being aware of each of her children and her fifty-eight grandchildren and those of her great-grandchildren who are old enough to be here, and knowing with relief that her family is now complete.

And I wonder what it is about this family that makes us come together so fiercely; and why, when we do, it is the inner remnants of *laughter* that we carry away with us and which above all things will linger in the days to follow? For the stories to which my generation listens have been wrung from a time of deprivation: one war and into the Depression and on to the second war that followed. And I think that theirs must be the kind of necessary laughter to which people cling and that sees people through so very much.

I remember Grandmother laying hands on our shoulders as we raced in and out of the farmhouse, telling us that if we were to come in we would have to sit down, even for a moment, or we would take the peace away from her house. How she would give us a penny when we gave her anything sharp; how she would scold her sons, my uncles, who searched the haymow for rotten eggs to throw at one another to relieve an early evening's boredom, and who also threw burrs into my braids—not out of meanness, merely as a diversion, and I knew this—and how she soon gave up the chase in the barnyard knowing that the time had come when the last of her sons could outrun her. I would stand between her legs while she patiently combed and cut the burrs from my hair, telling me all the while that she would "fix" those boys when they came in after chores, for supper, all of us knowing that she—and the other women, her daughters—would have so much to do between now and then, by suppertime she would have forgotten.

We arrived on the train at the beginning of every summer, first sighting the roundhouse* built on a curve of the cinder-chipped road, all tracks meeting and converging there. As the train slowed, we stood at the window just barely able to see the silver sun reflected on the roof of my grandfather's barn across the fields. Two window eyes stared back at us and then our line of vision was blocked as the train pulled into the station and stopped. One of my uncles was there to meet us and we drove over the unevenness of those same cinder-chipped and sooty roads we had seen from the train, past the pens where often sheep or cattle or pigs were milling and grunting and blindly lowing and bumping into one another. I learned from my uncles that these animals were intended for the slaughterhouse but I only half believed this as no one could tell me where the slaughterhouse really was. Only later I realized that my uncles had been telling the truth about the doomed animals, and even then I did not want to think about their entrails and their bloody cries.

My grandfather's land stretched nearly a mile, beginning at the dusty road that lay by the tracks, up the narrow lane that led past the spring-fed well. We had to drive through one wide gate, then a second, and the child who got out of the car to open and close the gates followed along with a running whoop so as not to miss the first greetings as my grandparents stepped almost formally from the house. Grandfather wore his dark-green fedorah, the same he slapped onto his head every day of his adult life as he walked out the back door. He shook hands with the boys and kissed the girls, rubbing our chins with the stubble of his often unshaved cheeks. He was gruff and rough and unpredictable, I thought, and it was only in the evenings when the family sat around the kitchen table, and when I felt safe with my mother near (she, after all, had grown up there and was familiar with the place), that I relaxed enough to notice the laughter in his eyes. He told us that when his children were small the youngest always sat on his own knee and was fed from my grandfather's plate. When the next newborn was able to sit up by himself, that child took the place of the first on my grand-father's knee and everyone moved along one space until my mother, the eldest, had gone past the end of the long table and come down the other side.

After supper the dishes were cleared away, and the uncles and aunts who had married and left the farm began to come through the door. We were kissed and squeezed and intro-duced awkwardly to cousins who had changed as much as we in a year's growth. Eventually, my mother and her brothers and sis-ters began to talk so loudly (and all together) that we children were forgotten until long past our usual bedtimes. Harmonicas were pulled from pockets and then there was dancing on the kitchen's green-and-white linoleum. Grandmother remembered to cover the canary, whose song she had never heard but which she loved because it had been a gift from her sons. We were final-ly trundled off to bed, following the smoky odour of the kerosene lamp as some adult led the way. Up the stairs we would go, to rooms that had holes in the floor for stovepipes, around which we daringly crept back and huddled and listened after the grown-ups had returned to the kitchen for more merrymaking.

Grandfather would turn aside to sing songs my grand-mother was not to understand; but she knew him too well to be deceived and as her foot tapped impatiently, she would say, "Don't be so foolish, Rory. Oh don't be so foolish." It seemed to me, even then, that Grandfather was at a lifelong disadvantage; he must live with the ultimate truth that his wife could, and did, win every argument, merely by turning her back.

When Grandfather had had three drinks of whisky he would sing, *If the baby she don't pee, squeeze her belly, squeeze her belly,* and *Kelly with the green-necked tie.* And my uncles and my father sang, *Come home my boy, your poor old father wants you, Come home my boy, your mother dear is dead.*

Sometimes my grandmother would attempt to get up from the table to prepare food for the next day but one of her tall sons would protest and waltz her around the kitchen until she would sit again. Her foot always moved in perfect time to the music by some means unknown to us, perhaps because her eyes were so careful and quick they could see rhythm on the cupped hands over the harmonica; or perhaps because she could feel the floor moving beneath the tapping feet.

We heard my grandfather telling jokes about his large straight nose: how he had never liked to raise it above the trenches of the First Great War. And it was not until I was much older that I realized how his cheeks had become webbed with purplish streaks and how his eyebrows had so thickened and whitened they almost shadowed the great nose. Two cords stretched the length of his throat and swelled dangerously when he laughed. He was beginning to have trouble breathing even then. Long after he had stopped doing the farmwork he used to sit much of the day on a long wooden bench under the trees outside the back kitchen. The tendons would show through the fine skin of his hands gripping the bench and he would breathe with short rasping breaths.

It is a far memory from the one that takes me back to seeing him come in early one day from the fields, complaining to my grandmother that he had ripped the seat out of his overalls. His two large hands scooped up the baking that lay on the table and placed it on a countertop while he flung himself down the length of the kitchen table that could, with some shifting, accommodate twenty-two people. My grandmother stopped what she was doing and went for her sewing-basket while he said to my mother, "Bring me my tea, Nessa."

He lay there on his belly drinking his cup of tea, his chin reaching over one end of the wooden table, while my grandmother sewed the pants right on him and the grandchildren stood in a semi-circle hooting and hollering at the spectacle.

Or in those same overalls taking us blueberry picking on a Sunday afternoon. We would pile into my uncle's truck and head for Stony Lonesome where the berries grew. My grandfather would seat himself where the berries were thickest and could fill an enamel-coated bucket before we could cover its bottom. When he saw that we were becoming hot or cross or tired he would take us to a clover patch to find four-leaf clovers. He would sit again, his legs spread apart, and to our astonishment would pull four-leaf clovers one after another from the ground until each child had been given one for luck.

In the mornings, every childhood summer, I lay in bed awake at five o'clock to hear my grandfather go downstairs to light the wood stove. When the kettle had boiled and he had made my grandmother's tea, I heard him lift the long poker from the place where it hung at the side of the stove; he tapped steadily at the pipe, which rose through the floor of my grandmother's room and she, waiting in bed for the signal that shuddered through her floor, answered softly as she slipped from her bed, "All right, Rory, all right."

I used to wonder, when I was older, married and having my own children, and when I was learning how difficult it is to share a life with several other people, if those few moments over tea at five o'clock every morning were the only ones in which my grandmother had any measure of privacy with her husband. They had for so many years been surrounded by children, I could only imagine them falling wearily into bed at the end of each day and rising before dawn just as wearily the next, to face more of the same.

My grandmother herself answered my unvoiced question. She sat with me in the corridor of the hospital while my grandfather lay dying, and she told me how she and my grandfather would lie in bed at night talking over the events of the day, that being the only private time they ever had together during those long child-rearing years.

"But how?" I asked, incredulous, thinking of the confusion, the demands of the children and even, more practically, of the dark—knowing that the farmhouse had had electricity only in the most recent years. "How could you possibly have understood?"

She took my hand in hers to show me. "Your grandfather held my hand, like this, to his lips and I read his lips with my fingers and I whispered back to him. And that is how, all of those years, we were able to speak together, even in the dark."

My grandfather and his sons were in the fields long before any visitors were up. Dick and Duke, with their broad rumps and sagging backs, were harnessed to the wagon to be taken to the back fields, and the farmyard seemed empty and silent when I and my brothers and sisters came down the stairs.

My grandmother and my mother would already have baked, and there would be hot cross buns rising like full bellies across cookie sheets, set out to cool, sheet after sheet, across the wooden table. A dribble of white icing formed the cross on top and this melted down over the fullness of each bun. There might be a row of six raspberry pies, the darkened juice from the bubbled fruit leaking out through the top crust. And a bowl of fresh cream ready to be whipped up at first sight of the men.

Lunchtime was signalled by the shrilling of the round-house whistle across the fields and I would by then feel sure enough of myself to perch out of everyone's way on a stool in one corner, beneath the framed painting of three cows, watching the men come in from the fields. The room filled with the sickly smell of sweat and my uncles lined up at the sink, which had no plumbing, to wash in the enamel basin, into which saucepans of water were poured from the huge reservoir at one end of the stove. They sat down after my grandparents took their places and the room became heavily silent as they reached for the food. There were roasts and huge pans filled with browned potatoes, steaming vegetables from the gardens, and gravy that was passed around and refilled from the roasting pan on top of the stove. Then the men filed out—even the uncles who were the same age as myself—and went back to the fields for the afternoon. The women began again, preparing for the next, the evening meal.

While the men were in the fields, my grandmother sometimes allowed me to carry a bucket of warm water for her, up the stairs to her room where she would wash. My grandparents' room had been built over the kitchen, which had been added onto the original house, and because it was lower than the other rooms we had to bend forward and walk down two steps to get to it from the upper hall. The edges and centre of the steps were smooth and shiny from so much use; linoleum on the floor of the room had been replaced in occasional spots by strips that did not match the whole. Across the entire end of her room (I have always thought of it as *her* room) and immediately by the two steps, was a long rough cupboard-closet affair that had never been completed or closed in. This held trunks and clothing and several shelves. There was a hole in the floor (as there was in every upstairs room), which admitted a pipe from the kitchen below, and from here one could kneel and look down to the surface of the large wood stove. There was a small table that held a washbasin and here I was allowed to pour the water and then hold the towel for my grandmother as she sat on the edge of the bed carefully and slowly washing each part of her body. She wore corsets and what seemed to me many layers of underclothing and over all, a brightly coloured dress and an apron that would stay tied to her middle throughout the day until bedtime.

There were two things that frightened me very much at the farm: one was Barney and the other, the geese.

Barney was the name of the watchdog that had always been kept to protect my grandmother and to warn her, during my grandfather's absences, when strangers were approaching from the lane. Barney was, in fact, not one but a succession of many dogs—each as it died in old age being replaced by a new young pup trained only by my grandfather. No one was allowed to feed or touch Barney except my grandparents. The dogs were vicious to anyone else but they loved Grandmother, curling gently round her feet as she stood in her kitchen.

During the time that our family was visiting, Barney was usually tied to a tree near the back garden and one early morning, while returning from the outdoor toilet and knowing myself to be alone, I passed Barney, speaking to him as I had heard my grandfather speak, and reaching out my hand. He, of course, bit me, my hand being between his teeth before I had time to utter the words I had begun.

I ran crying into the house but received no sympathy from my grandfather. He pulled me outside while my grandmother stood at the window, and he made me watch while he beat the dog; I have never forgotten that it was my fault that my grandmother's dog was so abused. I had then to make friends with Barney, my grandfather between the two of us, the dog and I staring, terrified, at each other. Barney had to raise his paw to my hand and I to pet him, and after that day and for many summers my grandmother and I were the only two who could go to Barney.

As for the geese, I was never able to conquer my fear. Every morning my grandmother had scraps for them—peelings and crusts—and one day she asked me to take these in an aluminum pan and scatter them to the geese in the yard. But those tall hissing fowl, knowing that food was coming, always lingered near the screen door of the back kitchen and ran toward it when they saw me. I jumped back inside and they cried and flapped, making a racket that terrified me and that my grandmother, one room behind, could not hear. I then opened the screen door an inch and pushed peelings out one by one which, of course, so maddened the animals that they became half-crazed. Then I discovered several small holes in the screen that needed repair and I began to push the scraps out through the holes while the geese reached up with their long necks and beaks and tore at the screen and the food. By chance, my grandmother happened to come to the end of the kitchen and saw, at a glance, what was happening. It is the only time I remember her being unhappy with me; she seized the pan from my hands and stalked out through the mob of geese, which calmed and followed her under the trees where she fed them.

There were times at the end of summer when my grandmother would come back with us on the train to my parents' home, and for these trips she would dress almost formally. Rather than the colourful dresses we were used to seeing, she would choose blacks or browns, and a *travelling* hat tilted to one side over her pinned-up hair. She wore stoles that contained hard blunt noses and furry claws and she imparted to me the wisdom that when I grew up and had furs of my own, I should wrap them in brown paper during the summer months, to keep out the moths.

She was very quiet during the train trips and we somehow knew that she could not relax because she was afraid she would unknowingly speak out too loudly before strangers. My mother would use careful lip movements, the two women facing each other across the seats, holding long and practised silent conversations. Sometimes strangers on the train would notice and would guess that my grandmother was deaf and would comment to mother or smile in a friendly way. But when people asked outright, "Is she deaf and dumb?" I would experience the quick anger that comes from knowing that someone you love and wish to protect has been violated, not realizing that was how the condition was then described.

"No," my mother would reply, evenly. "My mother is deaf and mute. Not dumb."

Once in our own town, I took my grandmother shopping. As we stood together at a counter I was suddenly shocked into pride as another shopper and my grandmother, with no warning to me, fell into what I can only describe as a flurry and fit of moving hands, fingers and fists as they recognized a like state in each other. The salesclerk and I stood by in awe as these two women held a mute conversation of hands; I remember the look of extreme pleasure on my grandmother's face. She had spent all of her childhood in the only school for the deaf that had existed in Canada at the turn of the century and there she had used *sign* language for many years.

Now, of course, there are machines that attach to telephones, printing out computer-like visual messages for the deaf. My grandmother will have none of these; for her, these symbols of technology have come too late. She has been encased in her own silence for more than eighty years. And she has long known what the rest of us take the better part of our lives to learn. That there is an element of self that can never be reached or touched by any other. That lone state, which is the element of survival and of suffering, of joy and compassion and pain.

We drive slowly to the cemetery, a long procession, while cars and trucks from the direction facing us pull over to the side of the country road. Farmers such as my grandfather has been, remove fedoras or straw hats, placing them on the seats beside them as we pass.

My grandmother stands at the graveside. My mother stands to her right, holding her arm. It is as if a useless event has just taken place; my grandmother looks as if she would like to fling herself to the earth beside her husband. And then, I sense her slumping; her head falls forward on her chest; my mother on one side calls to her brothers for help and there is a quick rush to her side.

But Grandmother extends her free arm, holding them back. She takes a deep breath, looks around her and her shoulders shift with that fine sense of determination we have somehow always known. Her head is thrown back, the reddish streaks in her hair caressing the grey. And then, she beckons: first to her children, who file past one by one. The sons and daughters, the wives and husbands of these, their children and their children's children. All of us pausing before her, alone, for a brief and private communication with Grandmother, spending our confusion, our sadness, our love, or whatever it is that we have brought to her to spend.

* **the mask:** used for administering ether during difficult childbirth in the first half of the 20th century

* **roundhouse:** circular building with a turntable in the middle where trains are repaired

Contents by Country

Credits

"My Name Is Angie," by Beverly Terrell-Deutsch, from *THE TORONTO STAR*, July 26, 1986. Reprinted by permission of the author. / "The Year That Chanukah Came in the Middle of Summer," by Isaac Bashevis Singer. / "The Third Moon of Tagor," by Louise Hawes, from *THE SCHOLASTIC VOICE*, Dec.1, 1989. Reprinted by permission of the author. / "Who Said We All Have To Talk Alike," by Wilma Elizabeth McDaniel, from *THE THINGS THAT DIVIDE US: STORIES BY WOMEN*, F. Conlon, R. da Silva, B. Wilson, eds. © 1985 by The Seal Press, Seattle, Washington. Reprinted by permission of the publisher. / "White Christmas," by Elaine Driedger, from *LIARS AND RASCALS: MENNONITE SHORT STORIES*, H.F. Tiessen, ed. The University of Waterloo Press, 1989. Reprinted by permission of the author. / "Babysittin'," from *THE CHRONICLES OF UNCLE MOSE* by Ted Russell. © 1975, The Ted Russell Estate. Reprinted by permission of Breakwater Books, Ltd., St. John's, Newfoundland. / "Big Brother," by Shekhar Joshi, from *MODERN HINDI SHORT STORIES*, G. Roadarmel, ed. © 1972 by The Regents of the University of California. Reprinted by permission of the University of California Press, Berkeley, California. / "Tayzanne," from *THE MAGIC ORANGE TREE AND OTHER HAITIAN FOLK TALES*, collected by Diane Wolkstein. Text copyright © 1978 by Diane Wolkstein. Reprinted by permission of Alfred A. Knopf, Inc. / "With Friends Like These...," by Barry Daniels, from *THE TORONTO STAR*, June 28, 1987. Reprinted by permission of the author. / "Sucker" from *THE MORTGAGED HEART* by Carson McCullers. Copyright 1940, 1941, 1942, 1945, 1949, 1953, (c) 1956, 1959, 1963, 1967, 1971 by Floria V. Laskey, Executrix of the Estate of Carson McCullers. Reprinted by permission of Houghton Mifflin Company. / "The Visitor," from *THE THIRD WOMAN* by Punyakante Wijenaike. Reprinted by permission of the author. / "Pablo Tamayo," by Naomi Shihab Nye. First published in *THE VIRGINIA QUARTERLY REVIEW*, Vol. 59, No. 3, Summer 1983. Reprinted by permission of the author. / "Appearances," by J.M. Small, from *THE TORONTO STAR*, August 16, 1986. Reprinted by permission of the author. / "The Collection," from *THE TRUTH AND OTHER STORIES* by Terrence Heath. © 1972 by House of Anansi Press. Reprinted by permission of the publisher. / "Wilma," from *WILMA* by Wilma Rudolph and Bud Greenspan. © 1977 by Bud Greenspan. Used by permission of New American Library, a division of Penguin Books USA Ltd. / "Sonata for Harp and Bicycle," from *THE GREEN FLASH* by Joan Aiken. Holt, Rinehart and Winston Inc. Copyright © 1971 by Joan Aiken. Reprinted by permission of the publisher. / "The Soft Voice of the Serpent," © 1962 by Nadine Gordimer, from *SELECTED STORIES* by Nadine Gordimer. Used by permission of Viking Penguin, a division of Penguin Books USA Inc. / "Making Poison," reprinted by permission of Margaret Atwood, © 1983 from the collection *MURDER IN THE DARK* as published by Coach House Press, Canada. / "The Three Thieves," by Geoffrey Chaucer, from *TALES OF GEOFFREY CHAUCER*. Adaptation by A. Kent Hieatt and Constance Hieatt. / "An Afternoon In Bright Sunlight," by S. Bruised Head, from *CANADIAN FICTION MAGAZINE*, #60, 1987. Reprinted by permission of the author. / "A Question Mark and an Exclamation Point," by Revaz Mishveladze, from *THE NEW SOVIET FICTION*, S. Zalygin, ed. Translated by Edythe C. Haber. / "As the Buffaloes Bathed," by Pretam Kaur, from *MALAYSIAN SHORT STORIES*, L. Fernando, ed. © 1981 by Heinemann Books, Asia. Reprinted by permission of the publisher. / "A Very Old Man With Enormous Wings," by Gabriel García Márquez from *THE COLLECTED SHORT STORIES OF GABRIEL GARCÍA MÁRQUEZ*. First published in *THE NEW AMERICAN REVIEW*. © 1971 by Gabriel García Márquez. Reprinted by permission of Harper Collins Publishers Inc. / "Day of the Butterfly," by Alice Munro, from *DANCE OF THE HAPPY SHADES* by Alice Munro. Reprinted by permission of McGraw-Hill Ryerson Ltd. / "Darkness Box," by Ursula K. Le Guin, published originally in *FANTASTIC*. © 1963, 1991 by Ursula K. Le Guin. Reprinted by permission of the author and the author's agent, Virginia Kidd. / "The Magic Chalk," by Abe Kobo, from *THE SHOWA ANTHOLOGY*, V.C. Gessel, T. Matsumoto, eds. Reprinted by permission of International Creative Management, Inc. / "Grandmother," from *TRUTH OR LIES* by Frances Itani. Reprinted by permission of Oberon Press.